Much More to Life than Services

– BOB RHODES –

FASTPRINT PUBLISHING
PETERBOROUGH, ENGLAND

MUCH MORE TO LIFE THAN SERVICES
Copyright © Bob Rhodes 2010

ISBN 978-184426-808-5

First published 2010 by
FASTPRINT PUBLISHING
Peterborough, England.

Printed by
www.printondemand-worldwide.com

LOTTERY FUNDED

Foreword

Change is uncomfortable and often any voice that eloquently articulates a new vision can be seen as confrontational. Bob's book may prove, therefore, to be an uncomfortable and confrontational read for some welfare professionals. It tests many widely held and well-meaning assumptions about our Adult Social Care Services but, as my grandmother used to say, "Assumptions are the mothers of all misunderstandings". She was a person who spoke her mind, just like Bob. This is, in part, an angry book but its content and purposes are almost painfully honest and straightforward. His belief in the possibility of a new way forward is both heartfelt and passionate and is informed by over 30 years of his experiences as a social care practitioner, manager and pioneer. The pages are laced with integrity and inspiration. There are countless gems of practical advice and guidance from the author and from the wide range of colleagues who he has invited to contribute.

Only a very small proportion of public spending goes on prevention, even though policy makers are placing it at the centre of their plans for the future of social care. Even less goes on developing the local social networks that offer the most cost effective way of shielding people from future problems. When it comes to allocating ever more scarce resources, commissioners of our public services seem to suffer from a collective amnesia. Even though they know that supporting citizens to generate their own solutions is a viable and socially beneficial option they continue to allocate resources on the basis of easily measurable short term financial efficiencies. Their error has been to erase mutuality from the equation and to relegate you and me to the role of consumer. As Bob points out, 'Humankind has been around for a very long time and our survival and flourishing has arisen from our social nature and the interdependent resilience of our families, groups and communities'.

Much More to Life than Services aims to cure this collective amnesia and asks our social care professionals to use their skills, resources and knowledge to help people to come together and 'visualise, plan and implement their own support'. The book is a means to an end, a brilliant and sharp reminder to bring about a culture change for the better.

Martin Simon

March 2010

Author Profile

Bob Rhodes is co-founder of LivesthroughFriends – a community interest company dedicated to helping people who are dependent upon 'social care' to 'get a life' and helping the people and agencies that assist them to be effective contributors to this outcome. Prior to that he founded TACT UK – an organisation that supports people with intellectual disabilities and often very challenging reputations - in 1991 and led its development until his semi-retirement (unrealised) in 2006. Bob has a background in community organising, mental health services, social services and NHS leadership, and social enterprise in the UK and overseas. He spent much of the middle part of his career 'managing change' and 're-providing' services for people with intellectual disabilities. It was in this context, "where the emphasis seemed to be on where folk lived rather that how they lived", that he "woke up" to the limitations inherent in services. He was Social Entrepreneur of the Year in 2003. His passions outside his vocation are rugby union, music and people.

Introduction

Much More to Life than Services is not the sort of 'how to' book that asserts that if you religiously follow the steps recommended there will be bread and honey for tea. Caring for each other is not a matter of simple choices. Indeed it begs questions of us all. Not least, in addressing how we might go about supporting elderly, disabled and chronically sick people in our communities, we are compelled to confront not only issues about arrangements for individuals but also about the sort of society we want.

So, in assembling this book, my primary object has been to encourage readers to think and reflect, to challenge their certainties, and to consider new possibilities. I set out analyses and proposals that derive from reflections on my practice as a human services professional and leader over more than four decades and from the wisdom and insights of so many folk I've met along the road. So it is, in part, autobiographical in that I have set out to demonstrate how sometimes contentious or controversial conclusions have evolved and more complex conjunctions of ideas and actions arisen.

A long and reflective career informs me that we neglect our history at our peril and that, in our ever more fast-moving and commercially driven culture, this is exactly what we are doing. I am also reluctantly and self-consciously compelled to conclude that some elements of *1984* and *Brave New World* are with us. Our political system is excessively centralised and citizenship comes a poor second to consumerism, being entertained and alienated individualism. We live in a society where we are frequently exhorted to be outraged and to pillory those deemed at fault, to insist that 'they' sort it out, but rarely if ever to do anything ourselves beyond, perhaps, making a donation or entering a big prize raffle. Those who want our money, our compliance, or our votes address us as individuals. Trades Unions and Mutual Societies – key entry points for political engagement and communal action in earlier times - have been 'modernised'. Local community groups, at the hub of huge swathes of informal care and social reciprocity, have been marginalised and attenuated by a contracts and targets culture that devalues the unprofessional and expects its world to speak its mumbo-jumbo and satisfy its obscure bureaucracy. The professions have occupied large swathes of social territory that used to be the domain of families and neighbours. 'All for One and One for All' is rarely heard unless we are struck by natural disasters in which case people look back upon those few days of mutualism, interdependency, hospitality and real care with fondness, but persist in their silos, the entertainment modules where we used to welcome our friends. Talk of community in a 'let's care for each other' way will evoke mocking accusations of nostalgia. And if you are regularly supporting your vulnerable neighbour (and friend) you would do your local authority a big favour by registering as a volunteer, and with the Independent Safeguarding Agency, thus ensuring that you show up on their National Indicator statistics – you know, the ones that demonstrate that the State is building civil society!

Hopefully, the foregoing indicates that this is an angry and worried book but, that being said, it is also an optimistic and positive analysis based on the conclusion that humankind has been around for a very long time and our survival and flourishing has arisen from our social nature and the interdependent resilience of our families, groups and communities. When the current bout of individualism implodes, and in the case of marketized social care I believe that we have already passed the tipping point in the UK, mutualism and reciprocity, and the good human outcomes that result from this, will reassert themselves.

Much More to Life than Services is about both speeding and informing that 're-invention' and maximising the impact of the overall personalisation initiative in Social Services by providing practical assistance to those who are engaged in self-direction or assisting others to visualise, plan and implement their own support arrangements. It is also about encouraging policy makers to consider the challenge of 'social care' from a societal perspective and, a little ambitiously, to suggest a reversal of their tendency to centralisation and dogmatism.

To this end, there is a concise *'How to' Guide*, outlining key considerations in respect of Self-Direction at the beginning of the book, and a slightly longer *Policy Guide* at the end. The detail for both is contained in the text.

I am also a strong believer in the principle that there is no one way of doing things and that, as previous generations might have put it, we all have to find our own salvation. The *LivesthroughFriends* approach to self-direction is a very good example of this mindset. I am told that it looks like a very planned and logical system, and indeed it is. But, as you join me on the journey that leads to our iterative and nearly comprehensive method, you will see that the different components were discovered and utilised in different ways over 30 years or more and only brought together over time as a focused self-direction toolkit. And all the time I'm on the look-out for better ways, inspiring teachers, challenging ideas, and more effective practice. For example, I started my career as a community worker and that has always impacted upon my practice. It is only in recent years that I came across the asset-based approach to community development and, as a consequence, am hardening up my understanding of how to promote inclusion on a much more strategic scale. So, I'm always on the lookout for ideas that strike a chord and open up new possibilities for me and I thought that it would be good to have a bran tub of different perspectives and neat ideas as a section of this book. I asked a lot of sparky friends and colleagues for short and stimulating contributions and you'll find these in the *Lucky Dip* section. Maybe someone will ring a bell for you?

While I write with passion and conviction, anger and concern, I am in no doubt that no-one, least of all me, has all the answers or a golden bullet to begin to answer all the challenges associated with how we care for each other in a post-industrial, growth-obsessed society. This is my contribution to which, I hope, readers will add their own chapters. *LivesthroughFriends CIC* is hugely appreciative of the support provided by The Big Lottery to the development and publication of *Much More to Life than Services*.

Bob Rhodes   February 2010

When the Stranger says: "What is the meaning of this city?

Do you huddle together because you love each other?"

What will you answer? "We all dwell together

To make money from each other?"

T. S. Eliot.   *from 'Choruses from the Rock'*

Contents

GETTING A GOOD LIFE
A <u>CHECKLIST</u> OF IMPORTANT STUFF
An Agenda for Change

My approach to complexity is invariably to seek a simple framework that ensures that I can distinguish the different trees in the wood. Generally, I try to consolidate the key areas for attention and/or action to no more than 5 or 6 key elements. In the case of self-direction and the planning and delivery of sympathetic support for people who need our care there are, for me, just 6 vital considerations:

⬇ **Strive to fulfil the promise of personalisation – focus upon the whole individual – Ask a Different Question – "What is your Good Life?"**
Amongst it all, check that you are dealing with relationships, financial security, opportunities to contribute, a place of my own, and safety and security.

⬇ **Develop and practise your creative thinking and problem-solving capabilities. Become more skilled in thinking 'outside the box' and in responding to what someone really wants and needs in a bespoke way rather than to the menu of services of which you are aware. At *LivesthroughFriends* we use and recommend the *Go MAD (Make a Difference) Thinking* approach.**
Useful Link: www.gomadthinking.com

⬇ **Life begins and ends with relationships. Make sure that the person you are helping has enough loving and caring relationships in their life. If they don't, do something to remedy it. This is not a quick fix. However, there is no substitute for heartfelt and freely given care and support nor for access to social capital. We practise the Network Facilitation approach developed by *PLAN*. Relationships are the foundations of inclusion and citizenship.**
Useful Link: www.plan.ca

⊥ Our lives are enhanced and made secure through our contribution to others through our 'Associations'. We need to be active in securing opportunities for the people we help to participate in all the 'associations' of community life – work, leisure, sports, the arts, politics, mutual aid, volunteering. It is essential to direct resources at promoting interdependent communities. We are experienced 'animateurs' who continue to learn – presently from *Asset Based Community Development* thinkers and practitioners, the flourishing *Time Banking* movement, and many small initiatives.

Useful Links: www.abcdinstitute.org www.timebanking.org www.beyondwelfare.org www.independentaction.net www.abcdtraininggroup.org www.realife.org.uk www.mike-green.org www.fieryspirits.com

⊥ Don't lose sight of the fact that you are a Leader. Lots of people have got used to being clients and victims, neither responsible for nor in control of their lives. Wreaking a change in this will demand your vision, all your personal development and empowerment resources, and your team and 'movement' building abilities. Nurture the animateur in you! Don't just light a candle, be the light!

⊥ And finally, a golden rule, when support planning start with and invest in the community, and then spend the rest of the money on things the community can't do (or can't do better).

Welcome

For starters, here's something of an overarching analysis. It won't be 'right', it's my perspective, my opinion. Each time I re-read this I'll reflect again and add or subtract something, amend, or fine-tune. Someday something will happen that will help me see the issue from a different angle. Maybe I'll be inspired and demonstrate a new solution. I don't know the future but I do have some insight into my past and the way in which my attitudes and beliefs, my priorities and my activities, and my comfort in uncertainty and reflection have evolved. And that's my point. Dogma, fashion, certainty and elites, in any walk of life, should not be trusted. One size fits all really means one size fits no-one!

The very notion of a welfare state – of social security, of public services that seek not just to serve but to define how we all should pursue our lives, and of social care – is incredibly new. For good or ill, human society got by for many millennia on the basis of other assumptions, these frequently being couched in terms of interdependency and self-reliance.

We live in a very complex and pressured world. A place of apparently unsustainable economics where, in order to perhaps secure low unemployment and continued prosperity, we are required to spend and borrow excessively against increasingly uncertain futures, to gauge our happiness on our consumption, and leave worries about the squandering of fast depleting natural resources, global warming and the threat to future generations, and our increasing alienation from both ourselves and others to the 'experts' upon whom governments depend on the odd occasion that they are not seeking an immediate expedient.

For millennia there was no debate that babies and growing children needed their mums, their dads too, but the sexes, for purely functional reasons, adopted complementary roles. Similarly, old and disabled people needed their sons and daughters and the support of friends and neighbours who saw in their lives their own futures. Contribution and interdependency continue to be fundamental to many societies, and persist in some rural and ethnic communities in the UK to this day. But, for most of us, I would contend that we are conditioned to comply with a global culture that needs us to work to spend, to the exclusion of all other considerations, but casts us aside without compunction or penalty if our efforts are 'uneconomic' in the eyes of (forgive the archaic language) supra-national capital.

Concurrently, the self-proclaimed role and function of politics and politicians seem to have quite radically changed. The language of vision has been replaced by the jargon of management. Social liberalism - the encouragement of local ownership, innovation and collaboration – has been supplanted by a control and command business mentality.

Centralism, brooking little challenge and reinforced by information systems and targets that enjoy higher priority than the activities they are supposed to monitor, dominates. The primary focus is on money and services. Governments are now in the business of spinning the idea that they provide 'better' services than the other lot. And, if it all goes wrong, or if they set inappropriate or unachievable targets, a toxic blame culture will sacrifice some 'culprits'.

There's more to life than services and, in succumbing to managerialism and an almost exclusively economic world view, our leaders seem to have failed to appreciate that there is an abundance of resource that they don't control, and which goes AWOL if they seek its annexation. Perhaps there are better ways of getting things done than through despotic management systems that business schools deplore but multinationals often practise.

This is a book about social care – a terminology I reject. When I started my career some 4 decades ago the language was **significantly** different. We did social work, community work, nursing or whatever we did. We were engaged in an activity, in a process and not the delivery of a commodity. In general, in the work I did – whether it was with children in trouble, stigmatized communities, folk with mental health problems or with people with disabilities – I was challenged to help those individuals to pursue their lives as sociably and effectively as possible in the contexts of their families and communities. We had few resources; most was tied up in rigid services that had little to offer, so we became skilled in knowing our patches, networking, building synergies, stimulating initiatives and, above all, we sought, whenever we could, to work with the gifts of our clients.

Make no mistake; I am not harking back to some lost golden age. Lots of people were warehoused in large and often neglectful institutions. Public and professional attitudes were often dire. But it was so much easier for progressive innovation and experimentation to take place and for a diversity of groundbreaking initiatives to get going. Government clearly believed in civil society and in supporting citizens to generate their own solutions. Action rather than consultation were still the order of the day. I recall, when working in association with the Community Development Projects (a Home Office initiative) in Coventry in the 1970s, the then Home Secretary, Peter Thorneycroft, insisting that it was impossible to insert a cigarette paper between his policy and that of his Labour predecessor, James Callaghan. 'Governments have been the well-meaning source of the problems of the sink housing estates and don't have the cure. The best way forward is to support and empower the residents to make the changes that will have the greatest impact on their lives', was the nub of his presentation. Unfortunately, as the work of the CDPs highlighted the structural contributors to the problems and called for different central and local policies and priorities, government jumped ship. A comparison with current contradictions, with government seeking to drive a personalisation and communitarian agenda in tandem with a casework-based system that seeks primarily to serve only those in greatest need, is salutary.

Similarly professionals seemed more trusted to use their knowledge and expertise to make a difference. When given the brief to remedy the problems of a resource for children with learning disabilities that had been centre of a regional scandal I was given a free hand, of course in conversation with my supervisor, to experiment and innovate, to hire and fire, and to engage with stakeholders to make progress. In making the hard yards, in particular dealing with a hamstrung personnel function, the Divisional Director expedited matters. The centre, amongst other activities, provided respite services for more than 200 families. During the long summer holidays when everyone applied for a break it was logistically impossible to serve more than about a third of the demand. So I called a meeting with families and proposed that, instead of offering a residential respite service, we would offer a holiday play/activities scheme providing for up to 50 children per day, 4 days per week – making better use of the resources that would otherwise have served only 5 residential places. The meeting agreed the proposal with few naysayers and we just got on with it and no-one suggested that I needed the consent of the hierarchy. They applauded.

No-one panicked about the occupancy figures. The clerk who received them – manually then – was a bit flummoxed but understood the explanation. I guess that this level of professional autonomy and accountability to the end users equated, as an everyday norm for those prepared to accept the brief, to that presently enjoyed by an elite of 'super-heads' who are appointed to sort out failing schools. One wonders if so many would fail if real autonomy was returned to leaders?

By the way, this wasn't a one-off. Previously I remember, as the Head of a Child Psychiatry Service, closing the in-patient beds at weekends as the multi-disciplinary team had concluded that the kids we were working with needed not to be 'divorced' from family life and that our real patient was generally the family. Instead of providing a residential service from Friday evening to Monday mornings, we upped our family therapy activities, ran confidence building events, got a lad with severe emotional problems into the county schools cross-country team, and supported families through the inevitable challenges, consciously seeking to build their capacities. Again I remember persuading, not least the staff who might lose unsocial hours payments, but not asking permission.

So, the motivation for this book has arisen from a gnawing and increasingly evidenced perception that, in the UK, we have been slipping further and further out-of-kilter in respect of the relationship between individuals, families, communities and the State over how we care for each other from the cradle to the grave. There are, I believe, huge doubts as to whether the market model of social care is, even in the short-term, sustainable for both economic and organisational reasons. But these concerns pale into insignificance against the impact of these policies upon our very humanity and investment in social relationships.

I will not devote too many pages to political analysis of the journey to our present situation but would assert and will seek to demonstrate that we, as citizens, have colluded or stood by while:

- The best interests of individuals and society have been increasingly subordinated to the interests of 'the economy'.
- Governments have reinterpreted their roles in terms of management of 'the economy'.

- In the face of the contradictions, governments have downsized their visions around 'facilitating a better society' to fuzzy unmeasurables like 'fairness'.
- And, having moved along the continuum from vision and policy to management, governments have become increasingly centralising and directive, demonstrating incredibly clumsy and uninspired dictatorship rather than effective and empowering leadership.

We seem to live in a time where everything is quantified and that which cannot be counted is devalued. As Wilde's now unfortunately hackneyed wit would have it, where we know, 'the price of everything and the value of nothing'.

The exponential submerging of all things beneath a melting ice-cap of IT has provided the means for the centralisers to accumulate information and, believing that knowledge equates to power, justify their attempts to impose universal solutions, systems and procedures while apparently unaware of or insensitive to the implications for turning us all into compliant 'robotniks'. Increasingly, in many walks of life, what is known and what can be done is limited by the foibles of 'the system'. An essential skill of anyone involved at the human services 'coalface' and hence with an empathetic, intuitive and interpretative understanding of a situation has to be the moral and problem-solving capacity to by-pass or subvert systems that, as I will demonstrate, transcend good and ethical sense.

The Prime Minister (at the time of writing), Gordon Brown, is determined that everyone, like it or not, should have personal access to the internet. He is reported to have said that access to the internet is, "as important as the supply of electricity or clean water". One has to ask whether he has simply lost the plot or what his real agenda is when we are told that the large majority of people with internet access, after its mailing and messaging facilities, use the facility for recreation, shopping, or anonymous or risk-laden virtual relationships? We don't get spam through our taps and sockets. We are not constantly exposed to consumerist culture, adverts, commercial and political spin, and 'live now, pay tomorrow' hype by our sewers (they simply conquered cholera in our towns and cities).

While I do not want to promulgate spurious conspiracy theories about successive governments being increasingly in the thrall of 'international capital', it does seem to me that governments have quite simply accepted, and perhaps even not recognised, that they are subordinate to a global and largely media-nourished culture of consumption that, by its very nature, is doomed to self-immolation as resources are exhausted, the system generates more victims than beneficiaries (it will be the victims who were beneficiaries that will load the tipping point), and the climate drastically changes. I will argue that governments might, instead of being proponents of consumerism, be better employed re-engaging with a little political and socio-economic philosophy and coming up, in association with us all, with some strategies for visioning and then working towards a decent and sustainable society. It will not be easy. Everybody - including our victims no matter how impoverished, disadvantaged or disabled – has been touched by the virus. We want to believe that science, technology, clever people or 'they' will sort it out. And we're getting softer – less self-sufficient, less connected (despite our virtual networks), less grounded and competent in the essentials of caring for each other, and more and more alienated from communal debate and decision-making (politics).

It is against this background that Colin Campbell and I established *LivesthroughFriends* early in 2008. Our goals were and are simple and challenging:

- To contribute to the evolution of the personalisation thrust and the restoring of power in respect of social welfare to individuals, families and communities.
- To demonstrate the necessity and viability of a wide diversity of initiatives to not only support people to successfully self-direct but also, and as importantly, to effect a culture change in favour of self-reliance and reciprocity.

- To demonstrate the necessity and viability of a wide diversity of initiatives to not only support people to successfully self-direct but also, and as importantly, to effect a culture change in favour of self-reliance and reciprocity - through local action
- To raise grassroots awareness of the opportunities on offer and support people and organisations to grasp them.
- To constructively criticise initiatives that unnecessarily retain power and control in the hands of public bureaucracies.
- To contribute to the emergence of a movement of people who believe that there's more to life than services.

Colin and I had known each other professionally for more than 25 years and Colin had worked with me at *TACT*, a provider of innovative, person-centred services that I founded in 1991 primarily for people with intellectual disabilities who had acquired very challenging reputations, until my retirement in 2006. At *TACT* we had experimented with individualised budgets from the start and, faced by very significant funding cuts, had piloted internal support brokerage and individual service funds in a very demanding Scottish service over a number of years.

At that time *TACT* was a test-bed for innovation, both in terms of support practice and organisational culture and processes. We had become a provider of services almost by accident. The organisation had been established to facilitate the closure of Borocourt, the 'mental handicap' hospital at the centre of the *Silent Minority* TV exposé. It was a commissioning tool designed to get the job done, remedy the initial mistakes and establish quality monitoring processes before fading away. But with responsibilities concurrently in transition from Health to Social Services, it was with hindsight inevitable that turf wars and disagreements, no doubt fuelled by our aversion to 'pragmatism' over issues we believe impinged negatively upon people, would lead to a 'simplification' of the post-closure arrangements and, amongst other activities, we agreed to provide services for, eventually, 17 people with big reputations.

As service specifiers we had been very clear that the people had been ill-served by practices based upon containment, pharmacological regimes, and behavioural management. We questioned the assumptions underlying grouping people who challenge our capabilities together where, as I wrote at the time, 'everyone behaves bizarrely, including (to any dispassionate observer) the staff, and bizarreness is the norm'. So we had canvassed for providers who could support these people in ordinary houses in everyday streets and secure their inclusion in their local communities. No agency had submitted proposals in this vein and we were offered the opportunity to realise our own specification.

We had accepted what seemed to be a very poisoned chalice and, privately, quickly acknowledge that, 'we only know how not to do this!'

However, we accepted the challenge to get alongside the people, their families (where they were involved or known), the staff we were to employ in the various schemes, the other stakeholders in peoples' lives - and to learn by doing.

It seems that we did quite well because quite early in the process we were invited to assist others to address similar challenges either as providers or as consultants. And we learned – as we continue to learn every day – and what we learned culminated in fundamental discomfort with so many aspects of the way in which:

- social care has been legitimised as business;
- regulation and safeguarding as careers;
- leadership and management diminished to little better than administration;
- social care is defined as services;
- the professions of social work and caring have been delimited to systems and rules-dominated occupations;
- the bureaucracy surrounding social welfare has burgeoned without benefit;

- and abundance reduced to scarcity by blinkered preoccupations with resources that can be controlled and hence poorly applied.

What we learned and appreciated during those early years, with this inevitably fuelled by our previous life and professional experiences, has been fundamental to a perspective that says that the State's role in social welfare must largely be limited to facilitation and enablement because, given its core legislative function, the soul of government resides in pedantry. It is in its nature to:

- over-specify when diversity and scope for initiative are needed;
- attend to the worst case when, in reality, the best case predominates;
- place more trust in systems than in people;
- think in terms of hierarchies and power rather than relationships and reciprocity;
- in assuming responsibilities beyond its capacity, to be extremely risk averse and hence seek to procedurally obviate this to the detriment of the supposed beneficiaries (and it doesn't work!);
- try to direct a prescribed outcome rather than facilitate usually better grassroots solutions.

The learning achieved on the road to *Livesthrouɣ ı* .

many and varied. As we compared our experiences witɪ,

literature we discovered that we were not learning novel things

but that we were, occasionally, applying or connecting methods

and ideas in new ways. Often our initiative was really to fashion

a new question and fish in new waters in order to land some

'outside the box' potential solutions.

Having set people up, in the small group homes that were

progressive at the time, in ordinary houses, streets and

communities, we quickly appreciated how much line

management had been cultured into care services so that

managers and staff alike seemed paralysed by needs to seek

permissions, take advice, request instructions, or demand that

someone else did their job because they were not able to take a

decision. My small team – just 3 of us including the Finance

Director – were permanently on-call, telephoned over

inconsequential things and regularly needing to get hands-on to

defuse and redirect behavioural episodes. We had done the

training. People knew what to do but weren't taking personal

responsibility. The operational policies were empowering,

liberating. Our Service Managers were skilled and motivated but

(with a few exceptions) insecure, made cautious by careers in,

we assumed and later confirmed, blame cultures. I found myself

telling people that, "We'll get nowhere trying to empower our mpowered clients with disempowered

(rotated marginal text) ...nds was the

i the CAN (Social Entrepreneurs) Network and

d on my computer to find that an organisation

tha. called *Career Strategies* (now *Go MAD Thinking*) had been sponsored to give away copies of their book on creative thinking. I got one, read it, and quickly appreciated that its core message was really about taking personal responsibility with the consequences of that being the reinforcement delivered by the much greater likelihood of success in delivering the differences that we want to make in life.

So off I went to meet with the author, Andy Gilbert, and his researcher colleague, Ian Chakravorty. I won't go into the detail here as we'll be outlining that in the *'How to' Guide* part of the book; however, Andy and Ian demonstrated how we can all be much happier and effective if we learn and apply the lessons they had derived from exploring how very successful people think. Ian had interviewed 200 people who had enjoyed success in a wide spectrum of activities and discovered high commonality in their thinking styles.

Suffice it to say that when we equipped managers and staff with effective thinking skills the message got through that we wanted our employees to own their work and - within the values, goals and intervention styles of our non-aversive and person-centred culture – to take personal responsibility and express themselves through problem-solving, support plan development and resourcefulness. We were clear that honest mistakes, within reason, are implicit to life and progress. The crucial condition of trust would be that practitioners accepted responsibility for mistakes and for remedying them. From the commencement of our intervention in the most problematic areas it took less than 12 months for out-of-hours calls to nearly cease. An introduction to effective thinking became a core element of our induction package and, having trained enough coaches, effective thinking training was cascaded slowly across all activities.

It has subsequently become a primary part of the training and mentoring we offer to people who want help to fully self-direct or to those who seek to support others to control their own support arrangements.

In a similar vein, the experience of taking on a project without any real grasp of how to do it – with only tenacity, conviction and can-do resourcefulness to fall back upon - also propelled us into a much deeper relationship with and hence understanding of the lives of the folk we supported than is normally the case for organisational leaders. I became increasingly aware of the superficiality and aridity of the day to day experience of most of the people we sought to help and, with help of the stories told by 'reflectors' like David Pitonyak and John McKnight, of the tokenism implicit in so many of our well-meant efforts to secure their inclusion. Securing meaningful inclusion – our main performance indicators then being relationships with people who were not paid to spend time with you and participation in mainstream activities that provided opportunities for contributing, achievement and feeling valued – was at the pumping heart of the organisation. We invested heavily in training, made inclusion the context of individual planning and service development processes, and I and our growing band of leaders - as we 'walked the boards' determined to inspire, enlighten and catch people getting it right - rabbited away with an evangelical determination to supportively challenge folk to better achieve our goals. There can be no doubt that, even when we grew too large, people in the organisation knew its mission. Being 'Bobbed', I was later told, was seen as something of a rite of passage for those who happened to be there when I dropped in.

In real terms, no matter how heartfelt my concern about peoples' essential loneliness and isolation, I understood their situation from a perspective of needs assessment and what services could do; and I considered myself pretty hot stuff when it came to conceptualising person-specific support arrangements. Despite a background in community work, I scratched my head flummoxed by John McKnight's assertion that I was flinging good money after bad in my determination to turn human services workers into connectors; that is people who successfully assist excluded people into sustained friendships and reciprocal community participation. We were good at this stuff and traded on our success stories. When I checked behind the hype just about everyone we supported did things in the mainstream world; classes, activities, volunteering, church attendance and so on. But only 15% had friends who sought to spend time with them, involved folk in their wider family and social networks, shared their social capital – who were, for clarity, more than acquaintances.

So I commissioned and helped design and implement some work to try to understand why it was that these people were getting the desired outcomes that the majority were not. We quickly found that some people had these advantages because they had never been divorced from their supportive network of committed family and friends. However, most of the people we supported enjoyed little or no support of this ilk.

We discovered that the people who enjoyed these outcomes without benefit of a family network enjoyed the patronage of, in all but one case, someone relatively senior in the organisation who had facilitated introductions and connections. When we engaged an organisational/occupational psychologist to profile the group, which included me as I'd been identified as the catalyst in a number of peoples' lives, we discovered remarkable commonality between the participants. We were found to have strong entrepreneurial characteristics, to be driven and highly principled, to be impatient and sometimes impulsive rule breakers or benders, good at influencing and persuasion, and very tenacious. Here were people who employed lots of strategies, networked and built relationships and contacts, and who were not concerned with how many attempts failed as long as it came out right eventually. They tended to take personal responsibility and not engage over much in recriminations and blame. They preferred having enthusiastic collaborators and followers rather than subordinates. They tended to see and exploit peoples' gifts and talents – colleagues and clients.

Everything we learned about ourselves confirmed John McKnight's assertion that connectors are gift-focused, essentially extravert, risk-taking, life-affirming, enabling and trusting personalities – not because they are any more talented or greater human beings than anyone else; indeed, a team where these people were over-represented would be more trouble than a wagonload of monkeys.

John suggests that people who are drawn to human services work tend not to share these characteristics. They perceive what's wrong and are drawn to put it right. They tend to a world view that is less trusting and worry about risk. Rather than enabling and empowering they have difficulty letting go. They are carers rather than facilitators.

These insights raised lots of painful questions. The McKnight-informed stance seemed to be that the trick of being in the ordinary world was to utilise the everyday 'chemistry' of neighbourhoods and communities. It seemed as though the unspoken advice was, 'if inclusion is your goal, I wouldn't start from here'. I had been exposed to John's scholarship because of our well-known experimentation with and commitment to ordinary life principles and, in this context, exploration of what would now be described as individual service funds. He was, at the time, very involved with Carl Poll and the *Keyring Network* and *In Control*'s early interest in the concept of 'community' forged an interest group that included agencies such as Tony Phillips' *Realife Trust* and ourselves. *TACT's* work was predominantly with people with intellectual disabilities and I had consistently protested, much to our Board's irritation, that I could not understand why - if the services' objectives were to assist people to be more competent, more included and therefore less dependent – contracts were written on the basis of increasing annual costs to reflect inflation in pay and prices. The pragmatist's perfectly reasonable response was, of course, that commissioners specified service inputs rather than outcomes and monitored contracts accordingly, if they monitored them at all. This rigidity both ensured poor value for money and inflexibility in resource use that, in turn, limited responsive and progressive support planning. However, the most important and least recognised or acknowledged consequence of this persisting malaise is the perception that the funds are provided to support the provider's activities rather than the best interests of the client. This systematized dissonance between the desired outcome and delivery methodology is most pronounced when block contracts are issued or, worse, beds are block booked. Of course, it all makes 'commercial sense' as can be witnessed by the strong involvement of venture capitalists in the 'care sector'.

As an inveterate rule breaker, who tended to recruit rule breakers of principle to key operational leadership positions, I had traded upon the generally tokenistic supervision of contracts and strident promotion of our 'achievements' to personalise the application of funds far beyond the clauses in our contracts. And in Scotland, when a purchasing authority announced that it was going to reduce the value of contracts by 15% over 3 years (with most suppliers giving notice), we had taken the view that the people we supported would be seriously disadvantaged if we shipped out. We therefore negotiated a *sub rosa* agreement that we would deliver the new budget if the council did not specify the service and allowed us to develop and agree, through internal support brokerage, individual budgets and support arrangements with each individual and, where such existed, their families and friends. The immediate impact of implementation was a 60% reduction in the supervisory posts that had been required within the council's original specification, that funded a significant proportion of the required savings without impacting upon individual outcomes, and, on all counts, better lives for the people supported. However, even here, we observed that people were more present within communities that fully participated and it was dawning on me that we were not only trying to help people secure ordinary lives within organisations whose own needs subsumed those of the folk they publicly aspired to help and in a structural environment that tolerated paralysing policy and implementation contradictions, we were also missing a trick. It seemed that whatever innovation or insight opened a portal of possibilities for people to reclaim supremacy over their own lives and those they loved, political and professional interests would find a way to ease it shut again. Self- and citizen- advocacy, person-centred planning and practice, direct payments, neighbourhood networks, timebanks, circles networks, and so many more life empowering and enhancing initiatives seem either to be marginalised or adopted, standardised and de-natured by 'public administration'. If you live in Wales and have a learning disability you can visit the Welsh Assembly website and download your 'Person-Centred Assessment' pro-forma!

John McKnight talks about "competent communities being invaded, captured and colonized by professional services". I found myself researching, looking for examples of initiatives like Keyring and Realife Trust that had secured, at least for a time, some mainstream acceptance of bottom-up, user/family/community-led and less-professionalised leadership and provided some evidence of consequential and radical change in the social care hegemony. More simply, I was looking for examples of decolonization.

I found *PLAN* and the *PLAN Institute* – of which there will be much more throughout this book – and was soon travelling, as it happens with Colin, to Vancouver to participate in a *PLAN* development workshop. We were not the only non-North Americans to travel in search of inspiration. There, in a retreat, we met Eddie Bartnik for the first time, the self-effacing dynamo behind Local Area Co-ordination – probably the most radical, long term, public programme yet to recalibrate the balance between the personal and public in social care – and he was there to learn, not in an academic sense, but through his involvement in establishing a *PLAN* associate agency (*PIN*) in Perth, WA.

I will leave the wider learning from *PLAN* to later, save for the most important point. Working with Vickie Cammack, Al Etmanski and a room full of family members, self-advocates and activists that week, we were introduced to the principle of *A*

Good Life or, for me, a mind-shiftingly different question. During its development *PLAN* had moved from asking, "What programmes and services do you need?" to "What's a good life for you?"

Vickie and Al had quickly recognised that when you asked the 'good life' question you elicited very different answers and surprisingly similar responses from most people. In effect they were asking, "What's really important to you? What really matters?"

> *You might like at this point to ask yourself, "What is a Good Life for me?"*
>
> *Limit yourself to no more than 8 statements and put them in order of importance. Then ask someone who knows you well to comment.*

They found, as everyone else finds, that when people, disabled or not, old or young, rich or poor attend to this question they respond quite similarly with the following answers dominating:

- family, friends, loving & caring relationships;
- be comfortably off – no real money worries – exercise choices;
- be respected as a contributing citizen with equal rights and responsibilities;
- having meaning and purpose, aspirations and ambitions;

- a home of my own;

- to feel safe and secure – with this largely being dependent upon satisfaction of the previous criteria.

What was immediately evident to me was that these were characteristics that are frequently denied to people in the UK who are long term dependent upon the social welfare system.

Our day-to-day experience, let alone all the research evidence over decades from Kushlick to Wolfensberger to Pitonyak, tells us about the loneliness and isolation of a disproportionate number of people in the care system. And there have been plenty of initiatives to remedy this – but all destined to become peripheral to a needs-led system that views loneliness as a consequence of dependence rather than, as Judith Snow puts it, 'the only disability'.

Similarly, the English and Welsh if not British needs-led approach is also means-led with the consequence that service dependent people are by definition poor, once their savings are expended if not immediately. And I could go on into a miasma of moaning and hopelessness except that it is quickly apparent, if you have the wit to see it, that in the context of unfettered self-direction and individualised budgets, there is the potential for people to really work towards achieving the lives to which they really aspire – if only we can help folk to focus on their take on a good life rather than a packet of money and a menu of services.

By asking a different question we can put ourselves in a position to problem solve, trial and error, action research and generally get our hands dirty and engage with the messiness and abundance of life to develop the life outcomes that we, if we are self-directing, and those who we seek to help really, really want.

We founded *LivesthroughFriends* to demonstrate a diversity of supportive strategies for those who self-direct. We believe that the *In Control* initiatives have been seminal in generalising and operationalising the self-direction agenda but that parallel, complementary, and independent non-governmental movements are now essential to counter the increasingly evident co-option, professionalisation and reformulation of the personalisation agenda by political and professional self-interests. Despite best efforts, it is all too evident that long depoliticized and no longer autonomous Local Authorities are largely regarding personalisation as their administrative and commercial business, a series of work streams.

Gloucestershire, where we are based, is not alone in excluding the voluntary and community sector from the 'Board' allegedly overseeing the process on the basis that this ill-defined grouping has a commercial interest. In doing so they are frequently excluding those passionate local forces who take action to ameliorate the lives of those the council excludes, often with little or none of the mutual funding that council's manage on our behalf, on the grounds that often large businesses that define themselves as charities compete for very large council contracts. The fact that those with the biggest personal interest are leading, often defining and policing policy implementation seems to go unrecognised or, if challenged, is justified on the grounds that the bureaucracy is accountable to our elected representatives. My personal experience as a County Councillor in slightly more democratic times tells me that this defence is risible.

In Gloucestershire we have been involved in helping self-advocates with a wide spread of social care labels understand the personalisation agenda and think about self-direction. They have told us that now that they understand the relatively long term policy thrust and have thought through a framework for identifying their priorities (good life) and developing their support plan they are excited about self-direction. An enabler of a countywide network of people with learning disabilities that sent representatives to the Partnership Board approached us to see if we would be prepared to offer, free of charge, similar input to this network. The request was withdrawn after officers of the Partnership Board indicated that they would want, in effect, to approve our curriculum and indicated that it would be confusing for people to hear something different to that which the county was peddling.

So, at *LivesthroughFriends*, we are committed to generating local diversity that fuels an up-swelling of bottom-up demands for the restoration of individual, familial and communal rights, and the rolling back of government and its agents to the structural activities in which it ought to be competent. We have no ambition to become big, national, nor celebrated. The seeds of failure lie dormant but ready to germinate in these aspirations. Our political aspiration is for people to reclaim their lives just as women and local communities have struggled to reclaim the night in some red light areas. This involves lots of people taking action. It demands a change of culture and any change of this order has chicken and egg perspectives. Turkeys don't vote for Christmas, so such a change won't derive from the professions and bureaucracy. It will come from people who influence and/or become politicians. And it will derive its can-do methodologies from the experiences of those who give it a go.

So, we are doing our bit to develop local diversity, disseminate success stories, inspire and support folk who depend upon the support of others, promote understanding of interdependency, earn a living without compromising our mission, share emerging 'technologies', and encourage parallel initiatives to our own – all with the goal that a tipping point will be reached where interdependency, self-reliance and a collectivist approach, based upon the activism of marginalised groups and their supporters, will inspire structural change.

I have arrived at this analysis from a frenetic, operational perspective so it is reassuring that academic commentators seem to be drawing similar conclusions. In reviewing the literature while writing this introduction I found a surprising number of associated conclusions, of which the following is perhaps the most comprehensive. In *Social Work and the Community* (2008), Stepney and Popple suggest, '...that this discourse moves the debate beyond the idea of one cohesive community to the collective struggle for communities, which are likely to be characterised by considerable cultural and social diversity. Transformative action implies a strategy of inclusion centred around collectively organised action in the community concerned at a wider level with the re-democratization of civil society.'

It seems a crying shame, in a society where policy makers and professionals so frequently claim an evidence base for their actions, that research and qualitative evidence is so disregarded and the potential and richness available to our communities is so ignored, distrusted and devalued. This seems to arise from an elitism that asserts that, 'we're the experts and have all the answers', and defence of self-interest that implicitly limits options for change and insists upon incremental implementation of new initiatives in order that those interests can be preserved.

I learned, by hard experience, when closing long-stay hospitals that slowing the process always benefited the affected powerful professions and usually disadvantaged the relatively powerless, be they the supposed beneficiaries of the service or the basic grade staff.

Our vision is based upon the belief that self-direction and personalisation hold the potential to make the world a better place for folk who need social services, but only if we can evolve a society that is more reciprocal, less dependent upon and in the thrall of government, intentionally and consciously interdependent, and aware of its own abundance. This won't happen through a 'plan' but rather in a society where confidence grows as a wide gamut of bottom-up initiatives are encouraged, seeded and nurtured – where (and this may not be realistic!) the machinery of government seeks to get out of the way, diminish red tape, disseminate information about success stories, addresses the structural issues that are really its business, and sorts out unhelpful contradictions (like the benefits trap for disabled people who could and want to work part-time).

The book that follows is a polemic about grassroots action and shares the information, knowledge, skills, ideas and analysis with which we seek to equip people who want to self-direct or assist others to do so. This body of knowledge and opinion is constantly evolving, largely in response to the perspectives of participants and others who are struggling with the same issues. Hence, I've asked a lot of other people – self-advocates, their relatives and friends, fellow practitioners and thinkers (the latter encapsulates everyone) - to contribute observations, ideas and advice. Hopefully everyone will find something that fits their situation within these pages.

What is Personalisation?

If we were discussing manufacturing or commerce we would find it relatively easy to agree a definition. It might be something akin to 'incorporating customer preferences and choices into product or service specifications'. And there can be little doubt that the understandings of many involved in the implementation of 'personalisation' are informed by this perspective which is very understandable given that most are totally and uncritically immersed in 'the Social Care Market'.

Demos is a very sensible, well-respected, and responsible think-tank. It is well connected to government and is said to be good at 'reading the runes'. So, when it established a 'market intelligence' project, *Understanding Social Care Markets*, to predict the impact of personalisation (specifically self-direction and individual budgets) on Social Care Markets, *Demos* obviously saw no contradictions in the following statements:

The government is committed to rolling out personal budgets across the whole of social care in the next 3 years. The scale of transformation is enormous.

Personalization will turn care provision on its head, because individuals will receive their own budgets and commission their own services – with the potential to buy things that bear no resemblance to what the local authority commissions.

This means great uncertainty for the organizations that provide social care because the demand for services is going to change dramatically. But providers do not know what users will want... At the same time, local authorities will not be able to plan for the transition without knowing what supply is out there, what individuals can get for their money, and where and how they need to continue commissioning.

(www.demos.co.uk/projects/understandingsocialcaremarkets)

The questions that occur to me include:

- If people are commissioning for themselves why persist with council commissioning at all?
- How much likelihood is there that social care professionals and administrators will consider my first question?
- Surely successful businesses in any long term market adapt by being responsive to their customers?
- Perhaps social care businesses that are not close to their customers should not survive?

Since the Griffiths reforms, successive governments have accepted and variously strengthened the marketization of social care while concurrently philosophising about often communitarian-sounding societal aspirations that, to many of us, seem irreconcilable with prevailing social welfare policies and practices. While social care bureaucracies have grown and social care businesses have flourished, grassroots community organisations have often withered and civil mutuality and reciprocity is largely ignored and undervalued. In short, it seems that everyone associated with politics and the public administration of our communal wealth is obsessed with 'services' and dissociated from any notion of the wider reality of society, community, neighbourhood, family, kinship, peer or interest grouping, and relationships.

It seems as though politicians have a gut appreciation that things are out of kilter but - as they have succumbed to the temptation to get embroiled in the management and implementation of public policy, rather than setting policy objectives, voting associated budgets, and monitoring performance and outcomes – have lost their ability to stay focused and impact upon the big picture. And we, society, perhaps seduced by consumerist preoccupations and our own dissociation from self-reliance and mutual interdependency, do not hold them to account.

Nonetheless, there is a consistency of political vision that underwrites personalisation goals that have been expressed through a succession of policy and guidance documents over the last decade and that might date back to Tony Blair's 1996 assertion that the goal of his subsequent government would be to, 'bring the people and politicians closer together'. It appears to be the case that big ideas, that might be realised in a plethora of innovative ways, are quickly constrained by those who cannot see beyond the market, services, systems and self-interest.

RECURRENT THEMES:

To enable people to:

➢ Exercise maximum control over their own lives

➢ Live as independently as possible

➢ Participate in society as contributing citizens – economically and socially

➢ Enjoy the best possible quality of life irrespective of frailty or disability

➢ Maintain dignity and (self-)respect

➢ Sustain and strengthen family life

➢ Promote and support reciprocal communities

➢ Participate, through co-production, in communal strategic and service planning

These aspirational or vision statements have, in turn, given rise to a number of explicit directives or policies:

➢ Self-Direction and Personal Budgets

➢ Redirect resources towards prevention and support for carers

➢ Redirect funds from bureaucracy to the front-line

➢ Support for the development of flexible and responsive services that people want

➢ Development of new approaches to safeguarding vulnerable people

I am pretty clear that the fundamental objectives of the personalisation agenda are not the sole business of the Local Authorities and realisable through the re-ordering and re-systematizing of their businesses.

Personalisation implies culture change and a radical rethinking of our assumptions about how we care for each other. In particular, personalisation implies a fundamental rebalancing of power assumptions in respect of individuals and those 'in authority', an enabling rather than a gate-keeping role for social welfare professionals, and a marked reduction of those employed by statutory agencies if the imperative of moving resources from administration to the front-line is to be achieved. That, in turn, implies career insecurity for many involved in the leadership of statutory social care functions and it would be a denial of human nature to conclude that the majority of affected parties will avidly and radically meet or exceed policy expectations.

Hence, if I were in government I would apply my mind to the challenge of delivering the various personalisation policy strands and would, I think, come to the conclusion that I would have to secure the buy-in of ordinary people and their organisations. And, as an experienced and resourceful politician, I would no doubt understand that, in order to do this, I would need to:

- Be fully committed to the principles;

- Be able to describe the policy in clear and non-ambivalent terms;

- Be seen to be grappling with those policies and practices that people experience as contradictory to personalisation;

- Actively seek out help and advice from grassroots communities and their organisations, local user and carers organisations, advocacy groups and the like;

- And back up words with actions and resources.

The wrong message is given when government doles out more than half a billion pounds to local authorities to revise their social care commissioning practices but devotes just £3,500 to each of 8 co-production pilot projects to learn about non-professional support planning.

A simple definition of the personalisation of social care might be:

> Restoring personal power, autonomy and responsibility to individuals, families and communities
>
> Believing that individuals and families generally spend their public funds entitlements more creatively and effectively than public authorities do on their behalf
>
> Investing in the generalisation of sustainable, active and reciprocal communities

And then I might feel the need to ask:

Why Personalisation?

They say that when you can't climb out of the hole the first thing to do is to stop digging. That is pretty relevant to the position we have reached as a country as a result of the commoditisation or marketization of social care. The system is the problem. It doesn't work in terms of outcomes for probably the majority of people who are dependent upon it. It is increasingly based upon rationing with the criteria for eligibility insidiously rising and, as demand increases in line with a fast changing demography, it will inevitably collapse. Meanwhile, lots of people whose lives would be transformed by a little old-fashioned social work or preventative coordination are often condemned to colourless and excluded lives until events conspire to 'elevate' them into the highest needs categories.

I've worked with a gentleman with Asperger's Syndrome who often tells people that he spent a decade in very expensive specialist care because it was only when he began to seriously self-injure that he became entitled to assistance. Now, with a self-directed package of support costing less than a third of the specialist care service, he points out that he has the support he requires but is only too aware of peers with far higher needs than he has now who get little or no help, and probably won't until they are unfortunate enough to develop substantial or critical needs quite unnecessarily.

To be fair, the system that gave rise to Mrs T's and Sir Roy's root and branch redefinition of social work in the 1980s was far from business-like. Hence, when people from retail and systems backgrounds applied the rules of their trade to social welfare activities they were dismayed by the lack of clear plans, objectives and targets and by the often abject management of human and financial resources. They were quite correctly flummoxed by the lack of timely and even accurate financial and activity information. And, inevitably, they connected this state of affairs to the fact that scandals and calamities are a recurrent feature of human services; as cause and effect. What they failed to notice, because these things are not easily quantifiable and associated with a systematized command and control mindset, was:

- the extraordinary diversity of social initiatives that thrived in the apparent chaos;

- the abundance of partnerships with, and sponsorships of, grassroots organisations;

- the abundance of natural support options that arose from genuinely pedestrian neighbourhood social work;

- and the scope that the messiness permitted for innovation and development, generally inspired by engaged rather than 'general' managers, who knew and were accountable to both clients and their communities, and enjoyed considerable freedom to vire funds and redirect people.

In short, their business backgrounds had not prepared them for an environment where the key resources are often not in your control; where integrity, hospitality, sociability, persuasiveness and influence are of greater import.

They also failed to understand that these 'resources' are, in large part, a consequence of an individual's networking, relationships and collaborations and of a system that implicitly values the integrity and resourcefulness worker and trusts the people and organisations in the community in which the worker operates.

Background

Social Services, unlike the NHS, has never aspired to be a universal, free at the point of delivery, publicly funded service. Due to its close affiliation with the Health system and its policy location within the Department of Health it seems that large swathes of not only the public but also people employed in social services are somewhat confused on this point. It is arguable that, in the overall welfare state context, 'social care' started off as a component of the 'social security' framework – a safety net for the poor and the vulnerable, and a social protection mechanism that has, in fact, consistently failed too many who are abused or at risk of abuse.

Prior to the inception of the welfare state compact between the people and their governments a large majority of British families attended to their own social security, according to their means, through their mutual investments of both money and time. People saved and insured with a plethora of friendly societies and provident associations against future health needs, the threat of incapacity, unemployment, funerals, and even Christmas. These generally locally conceived and governed entities were a natural consequence of communities grounded in interdependence – where people naturally invested in their families and their neighbours as the anchors of their social security.

This was no golden age. The inter-war years were characterised by significantly more bust than boom and both the working and middle-classes had it hard. Poverty and deprivation were widespread. These were the boom years for institutionalisation as both publicly and charitably provided orphanages, asylums and colonies burgeoned to house those most at risk in these uncertain times.

There were many people excluded from self-reliance by simple poverty and the deprivation of their communities. Hence, with a spirit of 'never again' galvanising the 1945 electorate, the Atlee Labour government was swept to power on a tide of social security and welfare state commitments. And it is my opinion that, over the next few years, 'the baby was thrown out with the bath water'. It seems to me that it was at this point that governments began to envisage themselves as competent to order society and that the whole political class re-branded itself as managers of governmental (less and less mutual or public) resources and as social engineers. In a sense the notion of a planned, centralised national strategy started to become legitimised at this time. Perhaps this was inevitable given that the key proponents on all sides had been part of a wartime administration that had *necessarily* limited individual freedoms and assumed arbitrary *emergency* powers.

However, whatever the causes and motivations, the rot had set in:

- Governments successively redefined social security from the safety net with discouragements to the 'feckless' as described by William Beveridge to an arcane and incomprehensible mechanism for the redistribution of wealth and delivery of social engineering objectives.

- People paid a much greater part of their income to government – before the War a large proportion of low-paid citizens paid no or very little tax – and legitimately espoused high expectations of the State in respect of benefits and services.

- The populace unconsciously and incrementally has ceded personal rights and responsibilities to the State, despite all the evidence that the State is not competent to assume and deliver upon its 'promises'.

- The mutual 'social security' sector withered in its interdependency functions and, in my view, degenerated into an essentially commercial activity that in time was characterised by demutualization and the chance for a windfall bonus for members who had themselves morphed into consumers.

- An unholy *de facto* alliance was forged between global business, that needs ever-growing consumption, and benefits and services delivering governments, that depend upon ever-increasing revenues from income and purchase taxes to fund their ever more preposterous offerings to their electorates.

- Governments - instead of holding the ring in respect of the overall welfare of the nation, attending to a limited agenda of central and structural functions, and coordinating, nudging and influencing in spheres best served by a diversity of players and suppliers – have increasingly functioned not as politicians but as businesses. Their attention has been upon that which they can control through taxation, legislation, and increasingly through administrative regulation. In assuming that people simply want services they have styled themselves accordingly. And they have unforgivably neglected, attenuated and devalued the societal assets that do not appear on the Treasury's balance sheet. In simple terms they have lost the plot, failed to utilise our abundant talents, and colluded with commercial interests that have successfully sought to redefine people as malleable sources of labour and consumption, ever more desensitised to our emotional, spiritual, and social selves.

- Hence, in a strange intermingling of Marxism and capitalism, our day-to-day reality is founded upon materialism. The possession of non-essentials to a comfortable life compromises our relationships within our families and communities. Our 'need' to work ceaselessly to have the things that signify our success and satisfy our lust for more, limits our time for relationships. Our 'need' for leisure to recreate ourselves following the debilitating effects of our demanding and all-consuming work. Our 'need' to take recreational exercise because we do not otherwise get any. Our 'need' for labour and time saving devices and convenience products to allow us more time for income generation and consumption. Our 'need' and, contentiously, 'right' to have it all. A home, a family, a career – no compromising responsibilities. It stands to reason that the classic British nuclear family with one or two parents in employment with 2 or 3 children at school will be more likely to be dependent upon grandparents than engaged in caring for them.

- Concurrently our consumer world is now quite bizarrely sanitized and professionalised. We no longer die in the bosom of our families – although the loneliness and anonymity experienced by many terminally–ill people in hospital is increasingly recognised. Lots of mature people have never accompanied a loved one through the last moments of their life, witnessed a death, nor seen a corpse. Children seem to be generally 'protected' from the process – and perhaps in need of therapy to resolve their trauma in the event they are unavoidably involved. Bedridden grannies no longer inhabit our front rooms, visited by old friends on the way to the shops, gossiped with by the postman, and using the commode when the door and curtains are closed.

- If we add to the foregoing points:

1. the quite scurrilous notion that loving and caring for others is a pretty demanding and low-status activity undertaken by people who lack ambition, are not successful enough to engage others to do it for them, or by the put-upon;

2. and that looking after those who have loved you is an embarrassing, messy, sometimes smelly, emotionally demanding, grindingly boring and socially isolating activity, on a par with a life sentence;

it is hardly surprising that so many of us, who find ourselves dependent upon others, assume the guise of an intolerable burden and resolve to accept isolation, loneliness and purposelessness as inherent to our condition and the bearing of it as the contribution we can still make to the well-being of those we love. After all, we are part of a society that implicitly places materialistic 'successes' above kinship, intimacy, duty and reciprocity, interdependency, self-sacrifice and love.

- In short, I would contend that we have moved increasingly quickly along the continuum from communalism to individualism since 1945 and have passed the point of sustainability, probably at the point of the Griffiths reforms. These were a radical, conviction politics response to what, to even the moderately anally retentive, would have appeared as the chaos of social services. Published in 1988 and made statute through the *NHS & Community Care Act* in 1990, the Griffiths Report applied the methodologies and terminologies of business and management to social services. Mrs Thatcher had asked the boss of *Sainsbury* to apply his business expertise to resolving what she perceived to be the fuzzy thinking and inefficiencies of both the NHS and Social Services. Mrs T might well, had she been so self-aware, have changed her Christian name from Margaret to Market as she clearly believed that markets provided the prism through which the solutions to everything might be viewed. She was in charge in 1982 when the Barclay Report was published. Barclay clearly described the messiness and complexities of social work and social interventions, highlighted the simple fact that the majority of support provided was familial or informal, and championed the generalisation and practice development of patch-based, community social work (underplaying, in my view, the role of general community work and development), and made it clear that social services operate in the context of society and required a collaborative, integrating and innovative style of leadership. I suspect that the report was dismissed by the governing coterie as yet further evidence of the unscientific and wishy-washy proclivities of linen-suited social scientists. Within 6 years the rules of the market were applied, the commoditised language of social care took hold, and the credibility of the already shaky notion that social services constitute a partnership between the people and their government was severely undermined. We entered an era where accountants and systems designers are king. Where everything has a price and, if you cannot count or price it, it does not exist and, therefore, does not appear in the management information upon which too many harassed decision-makers depend.

- Just as we are beginning to appreciate that, in the context of food security, people need a connection to the soil and an appreciation of where food comes from and how it is produced (more than 50% of UK food is said to be wasted between the field and the plate), I will assert that sustainable social security depends upon people being truly connected to each other, to intimate relationships, to family and to communities, and that a healthy and sustainable society depends upon a governing philosophy that recognises that services are very much subordinate to and supplementary to what caring human beings bring to each other – and that the role of government is primarily to nurture a kind and collaborative society.

Personal Autonomy, Individualism, Personalisation...

Personalisation, while it sounds like a term that ought to have had its roots in the human services world, is a business concept. So it is not surprising that it should be attractive to politicians who, while assuming the guise of business managers, are keen to square the circle and legitimise themselves as elected representatives, political thinkers and listening democrats.

In business, personalisation is essentially concerned with finding ways of tailoring production to the specific needs of each customer or, in the case of mass-production, taking a broad swath of customer wishes into account when redesigning a product. The assumption is that the likelihood of happy customers, repeat business and product loyalty are derived from engaging with customers, acting upon their wishes and encouraging them to feel ownership for the product.

In UK politics there have been parallel challenges and motivations:

o   **People feel Disempowered:** The State has become progressively more centralised, unaccountable and bureaucratised, and citizens (or should this be 'subjects') feel increasingly marginalized and disempowered. UK politicians have their roots in liberal democracy and want to be seen to be doing something about this.

o   **People have sustained Low Expectations of the public social care system:** The centralised State, with its burgeoning bureaucracy and managerialist tendencies (some might say obsession), has proved somewhat ineffective in achieving its policy objectives (especially when it needs to pursue these through subordinate bureaucracies such as local authorities) and hence its much vaunted services, both statutory and commissioned through third parties, are too often inflexible, not person-centred, poor value for money, lacking innovation, and frequently struggle to achieve and sustain basic standards. This is not a recent phenomenon. It has applied throughout my 4 decades in human services. Here's an example from the early 1990s:

The absence of clear and inescapable directives from government provides an environment in which those professionals who are unsympathetic to the thrust of social policy… have room for manoeuvre. Consequently, far from government policy being represented in a set of coherent and consistent practices across England, differing only in relation to local circumstances and individual need, it is represented in bizarre and piecemeal fashion according to the preferences of powerful professionals.

Jean Collins writing about the resettlement of people from Mental Handicap Hospitals in VIA's, 'The Resettlement Game' 1993 in association with JR Foundation.

Committed people employed to provide these services say that they are hamstrung by oppressive specifications, administrative red tape, and regulations.

o   **Put the money directly in peoples' hands:** Ordinary people caught up in these problem systems frequently assert that they could do the job better and spend the money more effectively. Government knows that this is true but does not know how to make it happen except through existing social care mechanism that will inevitably attenuate the core goals.

o   **To break the vicious circle of rationing:** The impact of the creation of a social care market, based to a very large extent upon the patronage of a public purchaser, has been an unconscionably rigid, uncreative and wasteful application of public monies. The impact of care management thinking, far from Mrs T's launching analogy of sensible housewives doing sensible things, has been to incrementally downgrade social work from a professional art form to a process concerned with establishing the extent of someone's needs and hence their eligibility for services, and having established eligibility, finding and allocating services within their department's specified cost bandings with approved providers through pre-contracted 'beds' or as spot purchases. Job done! However, given the public sector's undemanding response times, it was not long before it was sort of realised that the implementation of the notion that funded services might be the panacea for all social ills had an expensive downside. Instead of being, in the best of practice situations, catalysts and problem-solvers working with a messy palette of family, friends, grant aided projects, public money, charitable money, public services, independent services, statutory funds from a range of departments, and innumerable other resources, care managers/social workers became increasingly fixated upon their own budgets and the services associated with them. Inevitably, demand quickly exceeded the nonetheless exponentially growing pot of resources and that pot grew even quicker as infrastructure was built to control and manage it. Then, without any apparent reflection as to the reasons for the scarcity of resources, nor evidence-based research into the impact of the marketization of social need, rationing emerged. Of course no-one was permitted to acknowledge the reality of rationing. This was to be a prioritisation process, essential to ensure fairness and transparency in the administration of public money. In time the Fair Access to Care Services (FACS) process was produced, specifying 4 categories of need to be established by needs-based initial assessments to which we all have a right. The two lowest categories of entitlement were soon eclipsed by a widespread adoption of policies that only people assessed as having substantial or critical needs would receive funded support. Of course, the people at the coalface with applicants for help are usually keen to help and pretty good at filling in forms creatively. So demand has been only partially contained and the professional integrity and function of social work has been damaged as service leaders, who are increasingly recruited from accountancy, IT, or general management, increasingly direct and over-rule their supposedly professional staff. Anecdotal evidence suggests that social workers, instead of assisting people to achieve the quality of life to which they aspire, are more committed to helping people achieve the biggest funding pot they can. One locum social worker I met, engaged with a team with successful experience of assisting people to self-direct, reported his surprise at finding team members who discouraged people from self-directing if they believed that the person would be entitled to an expensive contracted service through the managed route, despite the fact that he believed that this would be to their significant disbenefit. Suffice it to say that it is now no secret that social care is rationed and rationed arbitrarily and unfairly. Government wants to change this, but as the July 2009 Green Paper so obviously demonstrates, remains stuck in the market mindset – still preoccupied with money and services to the exclusion of serious and radical thought about the nature of our families, communities and society; our lives.

o   **To fund prevention from existing resources:** While the commoditization and marketization (neologisms not of my making!) and re-branding of social care dealt a serious blow to integrated social work practice and, by association, prevention; FACS all but wiped it out. Community work, community development, community action, community organising, and community social work are implicitly concerned with prevention, with capacity building, with amelioration, with establishing and supporting community infrastructures that deal with things before they become too problematic, about non-service solutions or more often partial solutions. We work with a number of people who are labelled with high functioning autism or Asperger's Syndrome. Only two benefit from adequate funding/service packages to support them to pursue safe, included and contributing lives. One, who has the benefit of wonderfully 'pushy' parents, has just enough; his personal budget being directed at the meeting of essential needs but also as an investment in the development of a sustainable ordinary life. The other, having been ineligible for support - as he was autistic without a learning disability and hence disqualified by the first criteria of the CLDT's eligibility assessment – throughout a much troubled adolescence, ended up with a very expensive service when he started self-injuring and ceased communicating verbally. Following his 'escape' (his term) from a system that often seemed to pay lip service to person-centred principles, he is still receiving more than enough support at something like a quarter of the price of the service that was funded as a result of his crisis. In his case we can be very sure that had he had a modicum of skilled and progressive preventative support in his teen years the public purse would have been saved around a million badly spent pounds. With some of our current clients we have evidence that the very act of engaging with them and their families in order to evidence and secure funding for minimal/preventative support packages has given rise to life-enhancing outcomes. Graham also has Asperger's and, while getting to know him, we identified an escalating drinking problem that was having increasing deleterious effects on both his physical and mental health. His very caring family, and others who had contact with Graham, were to varying extents aware of but downplaying the severity of his dependency. Simple discussion of what we were observing and the depth of our concerns were sufficient for Graham, who tends to see things in black and white terms, to decide to stop drinking (we counselled him to drink sensibly but he decided otherwise) and six months on he is fit and well and will not countenance a relapse. For those who have forgotten, social work was not always fixated upon resource management. We used to devote some of our resource to assisting others to manage their personal resources and to organise their lives. This amounts to significantly more than taking superficial details and signposting ineligible applicants to voluntary lunch clubs and drop-in centres. I have a sneaking suspicion that government would like this to be part of the job again. With both politicians and their machinery still stuck in market mindsets, preoccupied with money and services, and wedded to the perceived unavoidability of rationing (aka eligibility assessments), there have been a succession of plaintive pleas to the social care world to find funding for preventative work by reducing the costs and hence workforce associated with processing the system. As explained in subsequent paragraphs, nobody should be surprised that these proposals have had little effect. My proposition is, however, just as challenging. It is simply that used radically differently and, using the current fashionable jargon, in co-production with the communities served, existing resources can be applied much more effectively with the outcome that a lot more people benefit and secure decent, ordinary, valued lives.

o   **To get government out of the firing line for the shortcomings of social care:** Government has pretty much exhausted the supply of people to blame for these chronic shortcomings and has ineffectively thrown money at remedies (most recently £520 million on 'modernising social care commissioning'). It's an open secret that it is the social care system that is not fit for purpose. However, it seems to me to be self-evident that the core weaknesses in the system are the overblown, self-perpetuating and expanding, and resource-guzzling central and local bureaucracies that serve it. And it is an even bigger open secret – from *Yes, Minister* to just about every prominent politician's memoirs – that effecting radical changes that reduce the power and manpower (workforce would be more pc but less ironic) of the machineries of government constitutes the most taxing ministerial challenge; one that few succeed with and next to none with permanent effect. For clarity, the foregoing statements are not to be construed as an attack upon the integrity nor dedication of public servants. With apologies for the clichés, we need to stand back to see the wood for the trees. Government, since it got involved in micro-management, seems incapable of doing so. I am tempted to an analysis that their lack of a wide-angle view is a more comfortable place to be, given that politicians regularly chicken out of hard choices, quoting 'the art of the possible'. Similarly, for public servants, who are human and therefore generously equipped with psychological defence systems, we might conclude that turkeys have good reason to justify and organise the abolition of Christmas.

○   **The Demographic 'Time Bomb':** Underlying all the foregoing analysis and opinion is a simple, undeniably accurate, long-appreciated, and well-understood forecast that should have been planned for more than two decades ago, with those plans piloted and effectively implemented by now. We have known for more than 50 years that there was a 'baby-boom' in the decades immediately after WW2. We've had growing evidence for nearly as long that successive generations are enjoying better health, more effective (if ever more expensive) health care, and living progressively longer. Improved maternity and neonatal care has massively diminished the mortality rates amongst infants with disabilities, and it is increasingly the case that disabled people can expect a normal lifespan. As a consequence older people who are both economically inactive and likely to make demands upon public services will incrementally grow in numbers to constitute a much larger percentage of the population; implying a concomitant reduction in tax revenues with increased demand on the public purse. Conservative estimates predict a doubling of demand for social care services over the next 10 to 15 years (by 2025). This is interpreted by one-track-thinkers as a doubling of public spending and a market expansion. With global capitalism fundamentally and, in all probability, terminally challenged by:

1.   the imminent exhaustion of natural resources;

2.   the anti-materialist implications of arresting global warming and securing the continuation of mankind;

3.   plus huge domestic delivery problems in respect of 'protecting' the National Health Service, funding State Pensions, sustaining increasingly unsustainable Education Service aspirations, and fighting expensive wars. Those campaigning for exponential funding growth are, I believe, going to be disappointed. This seems all the more the case given the national debt accrued from the bail out of the clever beggars in the banks.

Good Life and Society Enhancing Reasons

Hopefully you, the reader, will find some points of agreement with me about at least some of the socio-economic and political motivations that underpin the political class's attraction to 'personalisation'. For clarity, this is not just a New Labour adoption of an idea. It is also a key element of Tory thinking – not that I can detect much difference in the behaviour of either of the dominant groupings.

However, for me there is just one overarching reason for being ebullient about the potential of the concept of personalisation, and that is the possibility of restoring or resettling re-empowered people who are in need of help and support from a perversely incentivised and professionally dominated 'Serviceland' to real life.

Institutions do not need walls and the process of deinstitutionalisation still has far to go.

My excitement at this prospect is simply grounded. In my experience, people who retain control of their lives (or exercise control for someone they truly love) and plan and organise their support with a determination to secure those aspects of life that matter most to them – generally intimate relationships and the opportunity to be valued and contribute to the well-being of others – enjoy ineffably better lives than those who are 'needs-assessed' and 'placed'.

In asserting this I am not proposing no role for the State or the death of services. I am supporting the notion of a radically changed role for the State:

o   primarily as the distributor of benefit entitlements to individuals;

o   guardian of the 'safety net' – no matter what we do there will be folk overlooked, self-excluding, or abused;

o   committed strategic (funding) enabler of kith and kinship, interdependent and empowered communities;

o   patron for good things it cannot and should not control;

o   and crucially, attending to the structural issues that most impact upon people in need of care and support – housing, access to employment, access to education, and so forth;

o   within a sustainable vision for maintaining a decent society despite the real possibility of no growth or negative growth circumstances.

For providers the challenge is much more straightforward. It is to thrive in the context of a direct relationship with their customers.

During my 15 years leading and building a specialist, national, supported-living social enterprise I came gradually to an appreciation that our organisation would have served far more people had our commissioning customers been service recipients. This was all the more reinforced in the parallel work I did supporting service users and parents and carers to participate in provider assessment and selection. When submitting a tender and being assessed as a service provider we quickly appreciated that we were participating in a lottery where the key criterion was generally price but where, occasionally, another factor was at work; perhaps a determination to not appoint from the existing raft of contracted organisations. Over years, engagement with 'stakeholders' became a more frequent part of the proceedings but we had no way of knowing how influential this was. We usually sought feedback in respect of our unsuccessful bids and usually received a technical response regarding alleged policy discrepancies, lack of definition within implementation plans, or general concerns about capacity or existing local presence (so why were we interviewed?). Rarely, if ever, were we told that we were not the cheapest option nor, to our great surprise, did anyone suggest that we had tendered for something different to that specified. This was astonishing as I cannot remember a proposal that did not start off by saying something like, 'We have read your specification and have deduced that the people to be served really need the following service outcomes to be achieved... Hence our method statement has varied the brief accordingly.' In due course, as my organisation (*TACT UK*) acquired a reputation for experimenting with and evolving a culture of user-empowerment, I was offered many opportunities to facilitate the engagement of 'stakeholders' in provider selection processes. By then it was common for commissioners to publish the scoring system to be employed during the assessment. Invariably the financial assessment and associated bits and pieces outweighed the views of the people who would end up served by the successful candidate and I had experience of decisions taken where agencies were appointed who had been effectively vetoed by service users.

I am convinced that decent, person-centred providers will benefit from being able to present themselves directly to potential customers. This will be particularly so for local and community-based agencies. In my experience, people are far from stupid when making these decisions – particularly, as we shall be discussing in future pages, when they have access to commercially disinterested and independent information, advice, training and support. The threat to all this is that public authorities get involved and get carried away with their own agendas!

Businesses have been dealing directly with their customers for a very long time and there does not seem to be any shortage of the goods and services that people choose to buy. As an aside, it is interesting that presently social care commissioners and contractors are loudly asserting the need for them to manage the 'market' to ensure the availability of service choice in the dawning epoch of 'choice and control'. Concurrently, local authority service providers are being awarded, without resort to competition, low or no-risk contracts and social enterprise funds in order to establish themselves in the emerging (managed or exploited?) marketplace. No similar local opportunities are evident for user-led organisations, struggling but strategically vital community organisations, or independent social entrepreneurs.

We too easily, it seems to me, accept local government's assertion that its, from my perspective, oppressive commissioning and contracting procedures arise through its responsibility to be fully accountable for the fair and effective disbursement of public funds. However, nothing like the same rigour seems to be applied when local government (or is it the machinery of local government?) apportions resources and powers to itself. We need always to remember that the most powerful stakeholders in public finance are public servants.

I need to constantly restate my fundamental belief that the foregoing comments are not an attack on those involved in the machinery of government. That would be tantamount to criticising lions for eating wildebeest calves. It is simply the way of the world. Politicians, however, are culpable if they establish or maintain perverse or counterproductive machineries and systems or sustain or reinforce cultures and beliefs that marginalize and unnecessarily institutionalise citizens.

The personalisation, choice and control agenda offers a real opportunity to reverse the perverse impacts of the marketization and to attend to providing an affordable and sustainable infrastructure within which we can all enjoy social security.

It is a prospect fraught with challenges but, in my analysis, these are deep-set cultural and societal quandaries that will in any case have to be faced as adolescent and individualist consumer society faces up to the fact that the party has to end and more grown-up and sustainable ways of living need to emerge.

It has taken more than 40 years now for us to not yet complete the closure of the learning disability (mental handicap) hospitals and campuses. The next stage will inevitably take even longer and demand strong and always learning, but always principled and focused, strategic leadership. It will require inspirational and inordinately brave political leadership because it will require the dismantling of the existing system to permit a new culture to evolve. As those closing the asylums found, it is folly to nurture a new way of being while sustaining the old.

It will take courage to admit that we don't know many of the answers and to regard this as a positive benefit. It will take great courage and intelligence to pursue this in the face of the *capitalist*, blame-culture media. And enormous imaginative powers will be required to envisage and communicate a credible picture of a post-consumerist and re-democratised nation.

This is the challenge.

TAKING ACTION

Until one is committed
there is hesitancy,
the chance to draw back,
always ineffectiveness.

Concerning all acts of initiative
there is one elementary truth,
the ignorance of which kills
countless ideas and endless plans:
That the moment that one definitely commits oneself,
then providence moves too.

All sorts of things occur to help one
that would never otherwise have occurred.
A whole stream of events issues from the decision,
raising in one's favour all manner of
unforeseen incidents and meetings and
material assistance, which no man
could have dreamed would come his way.

Whatever you can do or
dream you can, begin it!
Boldness has genius, power and
magic in it.

Johann Wolfgang von Goethe

Learning from Experience

It is one thing to whinge and criticise; quite another to propose another way forward. I've deferred writing this for a number of years; asking myself what qualifies me to pontificate? Eventually, with the encouragement of lots of friends and colleagues, I drew the conclusion that, after four decades of marching to the beat of my own drum, of very reflective practice, a healthy cynicism about 'experts' and standardisation in the inter-personal context, and a propensity for action – taking personal responsibility for 'setting out', making 'good' mistakes, and remedying them quickly along the way – I was as well qualified as anyone, and perhaps better equipped given that my starting point has tended to be, 'We don't know how to do this, so who is up for sticking with it and finding out?'

Nonetheless it remains a scary commission.

A lot of the learning and proposals I'll be setting out in this part of the book have been accumulated over the last 20 years – since taking on the task of closing Borocourt (the *Silent Minority* mental handicap hospital), founding and developing *TACT(UK)* firstly as an independent commissioning body (strange that we did see ourselves as support brokers at that time [1991-3]) and then from the struggle to evolve as a person-centred national provider of services, and most recently at *LivesthroughFriends* where we strive to demonstrate the creativity of individuals and families and the abundance of communities – but it did not start there.

Suffice it to say that I was fortunate to grow up in a family where self-reliance, integrity and personal responsibility were simple 'givens'. Critical debate in respect of social, political, ethical and religious issues were as likely subjects for mealtime conversations as local gossip or family matters. With hindsight, I have always been what Christopher Hitchens describes as a 'contrarian' (in the Cotswolds they'd have called me a 'contrary 'un'). Whether that was a consequence of nature or nurture is a matter for others. My dad had all the signs.

As a family we were involved in our community; most families were. My mother's family had been in the area for centuries and were founder members of the non-conformist Countess of Huntingdon Connexion chapel. My father, an incoming Anglican, had been welcomed into the fold (as a natural non-conformist) and both my parents assumed governance roles. As I grew up I began to appreciate the interdependent and benevolent aspects associated with this apparently religious community. The chapel organised a plethora of social events: seaside outings, anniversaries, children's and adults' parties, youth groups, bible study meetings that took place in peoples' houses with old-fashioned hospitality, and so on. People provided advice and practical assistance to each other. A local accountant who was a member of the chapel had both organised a job for my uncle when he came back from wartime service and secured a mortgage for my parents so that they could buy a house in our village and return from 'rooms' in the nearest town within a year or so of their marriage. The chapel was a part of a much wider network of inter-relationships that kept an eye on older people, folk with health problems, and deprived families. Jumble sales were not just about raising money for the fabric, missionary work, or other 'good causes'; they were a machinery for redistribution of the 'good stuff' that was put aside by the organisers as they sorted and priced their stock to ensure that little Billy Randall had a strong pair of shoes for starting school and his older sister had a winter coat. This wasn't charity. Billy's dad would be first there with his spade to tidy up an old widow's overgrown garden or to manhandle the bowling alley out to the field for a fête.

Our community life was expansive. There was a similar and interconnected network around the Anglican church and my family, despite my mum's strong non-conformist stance, managed to be active in that too. The Women's Institute constituted another very proactive circle, spawning amongst other things 'The Evergreens', a club and support network for elderly people. My mother, aged 71, had just returned from her daily round of visiting the old folk when she collapsed with the stroke from which she died shortly afterwards. This was not charity either. The old folk were her friends and confidantes, who had stepped in and looked after my sister and myself when we were small and she had a serious kidney malady. They had been there for her at the peaks and troughs of her life, as she was for them. They were there for each other in the humdrum and banality of days. Despite our frequent spats we cheered each other, had time for each other, ensured each other our place in the world. As I've said before, it was no golden age and it would be daft to be nostalgic but, in so many rural and urban neighbourhoods, in our very understated and often shy British way, we took an interest in and looked out for one another.

The Reading Room, later converted into a swish village hall, was a focus for a plethora of clubs and activities, whist and beetle drives, amateur dramatics, and was the first venue for the youth, later boys', club that my father unilaterally (he then won the buy-in and help of lots of other folk) decided to establish because he decided that it would be a good thing.

Prior to this, as an avid sportsman, he had quickly become a leading light in the organisation of the village soccer and cricket clubs and an activist in securing a playing field. Within five years of the first meeting of the new youth club - equipped with a wind-up record player and 1940s' 78s, a bagatelle pinboard, a decrepit miniature snooker table, and some skittles – he had secured the support of the National Association of Boys' Clubs, raised funds, and negotiated so that a purpose-designed, stone-built club building was operational on the playing field.

In a couple of paragraphs I will be very critical of the NABC and of the annexation and neglect of well-established community functions by human services professionals so it is all the more important that I highlight and celebrate the exemplary role performed by that organisation in the development of the new building. Here they simply enabled and technically advised a local initiative; providing grants, guarantees, funding advice, design ideas and, crucially, encouragement to ensure that the project came to fruition. In doing so they made no effort to redefine the project, assert on-going influence, or set conditions other than to insist that any future disposal of the property must be to the benefit of young people in that community.

Discussion Point: **The funding and enabling 'authority' assumed competence and integrity in the leaders it enabled, their organisation, and their community.** *People were trusted to do what was right in their circumstances and the support agency made its decision to invest both time and money in the project on the basis of the commitment and determination of the project leader/social entrepreneur and those around him and on his demonstration of the need. It was never suggested that the* *project should be relocated from an agricultural Cotswold village to a deprived inner city area. Less than a decade later this would, for the first time perhaps, no longer be the case.*

The new building served both as a youth facility and provided changing and pavilion facilities for the various sports clubs using the field. The club went from strength to strength with its membership swelled with kids from surrounding communities, an enviable programme of outdoor pursuits and adventure activities, competitive teams and county representatives in most competitive sports, martial arts clubs, a performing and fine arts programme, and a serious community service focus. He led the Boys' Club, a self-realising volunteer, for 25 years; an often wilful, cantankerous and volcanic personality who, nonetheless, is remembered by generations of now not so young people as a person who created opportunities for them to have achievements and learn about teams, organisation, leadership, personal responsibility, self-reliance and interdependence. When asked about his motivation for establishing the club he always cited the benefits that he had derived from being a member of the Boys' Brigade in the great depression in Liverpool, of playing football at the colony for people with epilepsy and the friendships forged with people of whom he'd been brought up to be afraid, and of the hopelessness and dehumanisation experienced by so many of his peers who, as he saw it, had been brought up to be victims rather than helmsmen of their own lives.

In his early fifties, and I think sensing the early retirement that was to come, he explored training in order that he might pursue a professional career as a youth worker. He was told that he was too old. In my teens I had accompanied him to the fateful meeting at the NABC's offices in Bedford Square as I was precociously investigating a similar path for myself. Despite the obvious fact that he had, in practical terms, more community organising knowledge and skills than anyone else in the room, an impeccable track record, vision and determination to spare, and should have been seen as an asset (in their position I would have grasped the opportunity and thrust him into the 'hottest kitchen' I had), they were much more interested in me! I well remember, as even a naïve and optimistic 16-year-old, experiencing a fast-dawning appreciation that 'establishment' was comprised of professionals and 'front-men' who seemed to be, beneath a veneer of etiquette and positional importance, concurrently threatened by and dismissive of the fact of non-professional dynamism, capability and achievements; in truth, ephemeral and transient in the real world context. He had the train, they'd only got the ticket!

As I progressed in my career this analysis developed in a worrying way as I watched professionals (and I am one of them) actively seizing the territory that should be occupied by ordinary people and their communities and indicating that these were now no-go areas for the uninitiated, surrounding their enclaves with regulations and emotional barbed wire.

There were, I'm told, just as many paedophiles and psychopaths inhabiting the communities of my childhood as now. There is also no doubt that children who were out-of-sight in 'care' or residential education were at significant risk of abuse but it now seems a paradox that the majority of us who grew up in integrated and connected communities were both safer and more roundly socialised and equipped for life than can be said of contemporary generations. Adults looked after and out for each other's children and grandchildren and we were regularly reminded about the people and situations to avoid. "I shouldn't go there, he's a bit funny". If we disregarded the injunctions it was likely that we'd get a reminder from whichever grown-up had noticed and they would be likely to tell our parents. The consequences of this were vital for our social development. My contemporaries grew up in a community of people of all ages. We learned, picking and choosing as we all do, from experience and wisdom and not from the limited fare of inexperience, fashion and a commercially driven media that is the lot of so many young people for whom the dominant opinion former is their peer group.

There was an excellent junior school with an inspirational head teacher in the community in which I was raised. Equally solid ministers served both the Anglicans and the chapel folk. We benefited from two loved and respected GP practices and a couple of versatile and resourceful district nurses.

But...

Discussion Points:

○ **The community ran itself.**

○ **Leaders emerged and formal arrangements were formulated as necessary but, in the main, efficient informality was the rule.**

○ **People tended not to look to the authorities for solutions.**

○ **People expected and received a lot from each other, actively integrating less forthcoming community members.**

Learning Task:

Write a list of important social innovations that you know about. Don't make it your life's work, 9 or 10 will be more than enough. The sort of things I'm thinking about might include Barnardo's, or Quarriers if you're a Scot, prison reform, early responses to HIV/Aids, the origins of youth work....

When you have a list, do some superficial research. What happened? How did it happen? Why did it happen? Who made

the difference? Are there any similarities between the examples and the key players? What was the role of the State and the professions?

Please make some notes here and revisit them when you've read some more.

Returning to my story… or a small number of key events and experiences that influenced my attitudes and beliefs as my career in human services unfolded…

Having got so much out of the youth service myself and, in the process, developed personally as an organiser and leader (despite being morbidly self-conscious and inheriting my mother's tendency to gaucheness and opening my mouth before putting my brain in gear), I was single-minded in my determination to pursue a career in youth work. The short-cut, without waiting two or three years to be old enough to do an approved youth and community course, was to train as a school teacher and do the youth work option as an additional module. So that is what I did, leaving after four terms having learned that teaching was, at that age, not for me and that the youth option amounted to some placements but had less academic and intellectual substance than the senior members/leadership weekends run by my county association. Eight or nine years later I completed a post-graduate diploma in community work part-time while working as a detached youth worker in the Midlands. During this I became very knowledgeable about Marxist and Pluralist approaches to community animation, a veritable source of exciting ideas and projects involving anarcho-syndicalist practice, and quite a star when it came to mapping communities. As an ACW member I participated in the debate around the rights and wrongs of professionalizing community work – which the wrongs eventually won – and which now significantly informs my concerns about the erosion of 'community'. But I do not recall learning anything about doing community work from the course content. I did, however, glean a lot from fellow practising participants.

Having dropped out of college and worked briefly for the YHA, I moved back to a bedsit in my home town and got a temporary clerical job to pay the bills while I worked out what to do next. A part-time warden-in-charge post was advertised at a county-supported Youth Centre in the industrial suburbs of a nearby town. Following an interview with the management committee I was appointed just a month or so short of my 20th birthday. The Centre was on its uppers, had been leaderless for some time following some uninspiring appointments, but the challenge had been taken up by three or four passionate people in the community. Suffice it to report that I left a year later to take up a full-time job with a *Rowntree* supported project with glowing references and all good wishes. During that year the fortunes of the Centre had changed and I, as an incomer who travelled in on the bus and was paid for just a few hours a week, had facilitated this; not because of charisma, nor professional knowledge and expertise, nor yet because I had funds to throw at the situation. With the benefit of hindsight, and because subsequently I have seen these components repeatedly in the work of so many others, I am pretty sure that:

o   I just happen to have what John McKnight refers to as 'a gift centred, glass half-full' approach to life and work – it can't be learned and is not the ideal profile for many occupations, but it is for those engaged in empowering and enabling others (more later).

- I was experienced – having, despite my age, lived a long apprenticeship as a protagonist in an active community and learned about peer leadership and, vitally, the importance of trust.

- I had been encouraged to express myself, to get to grips with things that I wanted to happen – so had learned about organising through frequent experience.

- That experience of a spectrum of activities, opportunities and associated achievements, was invaluable in 'spicing up' the Centre's programme, raising the confidence and expectations of the young people, and creating a pride in membership. We didn't do 'entertainment' nor diversion, we did things - like a full-blown stage review - that were about having fun working as a team and achieving something special.

- Hospitality and integrity were taken seriously.

- Communities, like many families, are a constant setting for misunderstandings and fallings out – I didn't allow these to fester

- I sought people out – both members and community folk – and asked purposeful questions and *listened*; and then connected people. I was working in their community, assisting them with their vision, and a resource in helping them realise their aspirations. This was not a consequence of some professional insight, code of conduct, or best practice advice. I had grown up in an environment where it was considered rude, bad mannered and counter-productive to impose your will on others. Community living depends upon, as Martin Simon at *Time Banking* puts it, 'people being kind to each other'. Kindness is the consequence of real respect, real give and take, and earning peoples' buy-in to proposals. Rules and coercion elicit resentment, disassociation and discord.

o   The resources and funding that we needed to run the shows, reviews, New Year's Ball (attended by more than 300 people), equip a music/band loft, and enable a range of other activities were, as I recall it, never too much of an issue and were generally sourced through subscriptions or gifts and equipment loans from friends or friends of friends of participants.

o   I started doing things immediately. My employers and I knew that I would eventually leave for a full-time job, but I would have been action-focused whatever. Consultations and listening go forward much more credibly when there's evidence that the leader can make a difference. Reviews and planning exercises are too often the resort of those who talk but can't deliver!

Discussion Points:

o	Community leaders are 'born not made' – occupational training offers conceptual frameworks and the opportunity for peer-sharing but should not be a prerequisite for paid employment.

o	When recruiting for remunerated posts, it may be best to recruit with gift-centred and entrepreneurial personality profiles and practical experience and achievements in mind.

o	People who catalyse active and interdependent communities are an invaluable resource. We should be proactive in recognising them and backing their work whether or not it directly accords with funding priorities. The impact of their work is communities with the capacity to respond to a wide spectrum of social challenges.

o	Active communities are replete with resources and become skilled at accessing statutory and foundation grants.

o	People get things done and really make a difference. In general, the best thing that their employing organisations can do is to ensure that they enable responsive and innovative practice and don't unnecessarily get in the way of or procedurally obstruct good work.

The next twenty years, up to my founding of *TACT*, will be compressed into a number of vignettes; stories that encapsulate some of the fundamental lessons that underpin my approach to social issues in general. During those years I trained and qualified as a registered psychiatric nurse, worked with young offenders and drug users, operated alongside a Community Development Project with alienated and disconnected young people, led and developed a child and adolescent psychiatry service, was a trouble-shooter turning around scandal-ridden services for disabled children, managed an integrated learning disability service within a Social Services Department, and led on disability services in two Health Authorities, majoring on institutional closures and resettlement. During these three decades I worked with a lot of really committed and often inspiring professionals, and a fair few who shared neither of these characteristics! However, across the board, it struck me that human services professionals share a common institutional myopia:

Discussion Point:
Professionals seem conditioned to look for remedies and solutions to everything in the bodies of knowledge and skills of their own profession, or those of parallel professions to whom they can formally refer. Assessment is often, consciously or unknowingly, focused upon identifying needs in the context of the services, interventions, or treatments available. As a consequence fundamental underlying needs are often overlooked and effective and sustainable 'ordinary' solutions go unexplored. Professions, in marking out their own 'territory', have created unhelpful limitations to their real

effectiveness (in the closed world of peer review and academic rigour it is all too easy to maintain claims to unique expertise). In my experience it is the 'polymaths', lateral thinkers and 'entrepreneurs' of the professional world who break the mould from time to time, but not often enough to destabilise conventional and exclusive 'wisdom'.

So here are some stories:

Peter: A 14-year-old young man with cystic fibrosis and 'challenging behaviour'

Peter came to us with quite a reputation. His condition left him very small for his age and he compensated with a winning 'Artful Dodger' personality. He came from a very caring if rough and ready background, knew the prognosis associated with cystic fibrosis, and was inevitably fearful and angry. A life dominated by a life threatening condition, frequent hospitalisations and absences from school, and exclusion from so many everyday childhood experiences had left him with few friends. He was ambivalent about his family, his parents seeming over-protective and always saying 'no'. His frustration had fulminated into raging tantrums, self-injury, and running away. This was associated with putting himself, apparently knowingly, at serious risk. He had been admitted to our residential assessment and treatment service because his

---

family had presented themselves to their GP in search of help. He had referred on to the Child Psychiatrist. He struck me as typical of so many of the children we saw. Had his family sought help from the school or social services it was highly likely that the label applied and the services offered would have been very different. I was increasingly aware of this because it was part of my job to seek to integrate the disciplines that populated the Child Guidance system. When I had taken over the management of the service it seemed to me that its implicit, but unacknowledged, job was to take over the parenting of our young patients, develop ways of managing then reducing and hopefully extinguishing the presenting problems, share these tips with their families, and then restore them to largely the same circumstances as those from which they had come. Of the three referring or supervising psychiatrists, one was training in family therapy so her patients tended to need family therapy, another came for an afternoon of tea and gentle updating once a week, and the third learned a lot from his discussions with us and maybe turned out well.

I had quickly come to the conclusion that the role of the service, wherever possible, was to work with both the child/young person and the family with the goal of enabling both to function more effectively and happily, and for progress to be sustained. One of the steps I introduced was to close the residential service at weekends in order to ensure that kids and families were not alienated. Service staff worked out on the patch at weekends doing family work, group work and running events.

It was a very cold winter, there had been a heavy snowfall and the canal that bordered three sides of the hospital was frozen. Peter had gone home for the weekend. On the Saturday morning I was called. Peter had done a runner during the night after a torrid evening at home. Staff at the hospital believed that he was hiding in outbuildings there. I went to investigate, followed footprints in the snow, and, as I got near, Peter broke cover from a shed and ran for it. I knew Peter well enough to know that a hell for leather pursuit would only make things worse, so I followed him quietly and tried to persuade him that it was in his best interests to join me for a hot drink, a warm room and a chat. It seemed that the matter was played out when one of my colleagues, who had also been called and had been visiting a family, burst noisily onto the scene. Peter was spooked and set off at pace towards the frozen canal. Fearful that he would fall through the ice I and my much more athletic colleague sprinted in pursuit but this tiny 14-year-old was more than a match for us and, to our amazement and then relief, reached the ice well ahead of us and kept going... to the other side, where he kept running. He was picked up by a police patrol car just 40 minutes later and three and a half miles away having crossed three miles of snowy, roadless countryside.

The following week the newsletter of the county association of boys' clubs arrived. I had affiliated the service to all the local children's and youth umbrella organisations in order to ensure that we were able to access the opportunities and facilities they provided both in terms of service activities and individual support plans. Amongst the papers were entry forms for the County Cross Country Championships. This would also be a trial for the County Team to compete in the national championships at Keele. We had noticed that Peter was almost desperate for recognition. The education unit staff could not fault him on effort, he committed himself to group activities and the often very competitive football session that had become, for the boys at least, a daily end of school ritual. He basked in our appreciation of his effort but he and we knew that he was not graced with ball skills. So I took him on one side and showed him the entry form. Was he up for it? He was ebullient and announced that he was going to run for the county. I expected opposition from colleagues, doctors and most of all his mum and dad. Surely there was a chance that this would put him in hospital or worse? But none was forthcoming and his family was there to cheer him on in the rain and mud of the county event. Success for me would have been Peter completing the race and not coming last. But not for Peter. He came a clear fourth and bristled with pride. By the time we got to Trentham Gardens and the nationals Peter was back at home full-time, back in school, and participating in a number of activities in his spare time including a judo club. He had quite a following of friends and family, and us, as he finished strongly in mid-field and contributed to creditable team result.

At the time it felt like kismet but, with hindsight, it is clear that I was ordering things to allow for this kind of serendipity. By making the ordinary world a part of the armoury of our specialist service I was opening up possibilities that most professionals deny to both themselves and their clients and acknowledging that human needs are usually pretty simple and satisfied in ordinary ways.

Rick: Big and hyperactive – too much to manage?

Rick is big and boisterous – 6 feet seven and described as severely learning disabled and hyperactive. In the mid 1980s the hospital that had been his home since his early teens was closing. He was 24. Contact with his family had ceased more than a decade before and their whereabouts were unknown. Many staff at the hospital were intimidated by his size and, having spent many hours in participant observation, his resettlement worker concluded that this, rather than his behaviour, had contributed to his 'very challenging' reputation. She described him as boisterous, loud, uninhibited, unaware of personal space, 'a bit of a handful', but friendly and fun. His hyperactivity was real and he was constantly on the go between hastily consumed meals, walking the hospital grounds in all weathers and wearing tracks into ward carpets when 'confined' indoors. When 'compatibility' was explored nobody named Rick on their list of preferred flatmates and it was decided that Rick should have his own place, with 'plenty of space', and a one-to-one staff team.

He moved to a semi-detached suburban house with a decent garden, access to parks and country walks, and within weeks both he and his staff team were at their wit's end. In the hospital Rick had paced the grounds unsupervised. In the town he wanted to be out all the time, was agitated 'like a caged animal' when this wish was frustrated, and resorted to playing his music system at full volume. Sometime in the past Ricky had been introduced to 'metal' and he loved it. His kind and generous neighbours did not. His supporters were exhausted – spending most of each shift struggling to keep up as Rick strode through parks, shopping centres, river walks and country paths – and frustrated and de-motivated, seeing little possibility for improvement.

At a 'crisis meeting' it was suggested that it might be helpful to be clear about the main objectives for the support team in their work with Ricky. They were clear that they did not want to be his 'gaolers' and that if control and safety were to be the focus the service would be letting him down. They then concluded that their interim goals would be to:

o   help Rick get involved in purposeful activities that he wanted to do;

o   and to assist him to have friends and allies.

A brainstorming exercise elicited more than 40 possible ideas and the team prioritised several that would be tried first. Amongst these was the idea of joining a rambling group. A group that walked on Wednesdays was identified, approached, and Rick was invited to join. The group was largely comprised of retired people who had shared their enjoyment of the countryside for many years. They operated a car-pooling scheme and Rick was able to contribute as he had a mobility scheme car. Things went pretty well and group members seemed to model their dealings with Rick in accord with the ordinary, respectful and reciprocal way in which his supporters framed their relationships with him. However, it was impossible to overlook the fact that Rick and his stressed supporter spent most rambles far in front of everyone else, with the staff member seeking diversions in order that the main body caught up. A feeling of belonging was developing, but mainly around pub lunches and the car journeys. While continuing involvement with the Wednesday group the team cast around for another group of quicker walkers! A group that walked at weekends and had a few younger members welcomed Rick. While they usually walked on Sundays they occasionally headed off further afield for strenuous long weekends staying in B&Bs and Youth Hostels. These occasional weekends with, to begin with, two staff participating instead of one, gave Rick the opportunity to demonstrate that he could adapt to comply with ordinary social expectations.

Several months later kind providence intervened. It was a Wednesday and the member of staff supporting a nearby group home had been taken ill. Rick's supporter was popping backwards and forwards holding the fort until cover was arranged. It wasn't Rick's turn to provide transport and, with so much going on, the supporter had overlooked letting anyone know that they would not be going today. So the car and driver arrived and when the situation was explained to him he asked why Rick could not come anyway? The support worker confessed that he could not think of a plausible reason but that he would need the permission of his manager. Fortunately, the manager was immediately contactable and - given that Rick was keen to go, knew the rambler well, contact information was exchanged, and a return time agreed – Rick spent a day without professional supervision for the first time in more than a decade. The day clearly went well and staff were told how the ramblers had enjoyed collaborating to help Rick make the most of the day. Soon after, Rick started to receive invitations to social events, birthday parties and for Sunday lunch. At a subsequent staff meeting it was decided that staff would be less available to 'support' Rick when he went out with the rambling club. They were alive to the fact that they constituted a buffer between Rick and 'lay people' and were quite a deterrent to the growth of friendships. As they stood back more it was clear that Rick's friendships strengthened with, several years later, a long weekend in the mountains with the weekend group without any staff involvement.

After about six months of 'strategic unavailability', the team 'came clean' with both rambling clubs and sought assurances that they were not exploiting nice peoples' better natures. They received those assurances in spades and many of the relationships forged then have stood the test of time.

This is far from the end of Rick's story. There will be more in the section on effective thinking.

Respite Care: A problem shared... and the power of asking

I tell this simple story in the knowledge that I may be accused of asking my granny to suck eggs. It highlights an ever more common problem as systems, procedures and designated authorities are substituted for professional judgement and direct accountability to the people served in our control and command partial democracy.

I had accepted the challenge of turning around a social services residential centre for children with learning disabilities following a major neglect scandal in the late 1970s. Its primary function should have been to provide respite support for families in the district with more than two hundred children on the register. However, it is in the nature of things that institutional 'beds' attract long-term occupants and here was no different. Six of the 14 places were taken up with full-time residents. Three more had been allocated to young people who had been hurriedly removed from an independent home where they had been subjected to physical, emotional and sexual abuse and neglect. They had been brutalised and were at that time very distressed and needy. This left 5 beds for respite care.

When I arrived the centre was run as one – a scary snake-pit as far as I was concerned. It was chaotic. Over the first weeks I got to grips with creating three discrete and autonomous homes in the centre and creating three dedicated support teams, each with a competent leader. Gradually we made progress and, for the long term children in particular, things started to improve with the initiation of progressive plans and first steps towards developing fostering and adoption options, including a family placement respite service in association with a voluntary organisation. But for the immediate future there were no quick fixes and the long summer school holidays were imminent. Historically, respite nights had been booked on a first come, first served basis favouring organised families and very often to the disadvantage of those in the greatest need. I had suspended bookings beyond those already accepted (we were booked solid for several months, despite the awfulness of the service – perhaps desperate people are not too choosy?) soon after my arrival while I explored the most effective and equitable ways of allocating resources through social events, questionnaires and chats with parents when they dropped off or collected their children.

In not too long I came up with proposals:

o   We would ask people to confirm their respite needs to us annually.

o   We defined respite as planned time when both the child and the carers would benefit from rest and recreation.

o   We specified the usual booking spans as Monday to

Friday or Friday to Monday.

o   Taking account of special requests, we would allo
respite episodes as a mixture of school week and week
sessions throughout the year.

o   Families would be able to plan in advance agai
known arrangements.

o   Children would normally receive respite care with t
same group of children. We would seek to group in order th
the kids were with friends with whom they might enjoy simil
activities. We would organise to avoid the possibility of frail an
vulnerable children being cared for alongside over-boisterou
or behaviourally challenging peers.

o   It was proposed that residential respite would be
suspended during the long summer holidays and replaced with
a day activities programme.

o   All children on our register would have an entitlement
of 15 activity days over the period. We retained the discretion
to offer more where circumstances dictated.

o   I proposed that the location for respite would not
always be the Centre. Youth hostelling, camping and activity
centres would also be used.

o   Similarly, there would be scope to provide sessional
respite in family homes via outreach workers.

o   Capacity would be retained to ensure responsiveness to
emergencies.

I approached meetings with families on these proposals with considerable anxiety and was relieved to find that most people welcomed them, all agreed to give it a go, and we were given a clear steer to implement. It did not occur to me to seek departmental approval for the changes I made and the first official response came months later from the section that kept the bed occupancy statistics, gently enquiring about returns that recorded 5 unoccupied beds for 6 weeks but more than 120 children served each week. I responded and heard no more until a note from the Social Services' Chair arrived on the Divisional Director's desk that enquired as to who had 'waved a magic wand over the service'. I doubt that the magic would have survived today's permission culture by the time everybody had had their say and left their mark!

Malcolm: A rugby tale.

I don't suppose that anyone has ever enquired about what Malcolm's idea of a good life would be. Excluded from day services he spends most of his life in a small specialist service that, I'm told, is a barren and deprived environment of unbreakable glass and bolted-down furnishings. It is apparently no fun working with Malcolm there – he and his carers have the bruises, physical and psychological, to prove it. He is a very big man and folk are frightened of him.

But Malcolm is not excluded from the sports inclusion scheme run at his local rugby club by a small band of enthusiastic volunteers on a Monday evening. He is six feet and a lot and Jim who runs the sessions, a rugby man for all his six decades, a rotund five feet four. Malcolm is 'delivered' by two support staff who often retire to the bar for what I'm sure they perceive as deserved respite.

Jim is no respecter of reputations. Jim and Malcolm are mates who delight in each other's company. I would hazard that Jim is the first person that Malcolm has met in a long time who is not frightened of him. Jim expects that his enthusiasm, warmth and trust will be reciprocated. Crucially, Jim makes few demands on Malcolm – and, when he does, he makes it fun. From their first meeting Jim has expected the best from Malcolm and he is usually rewarded. When he isn't, Jim just carries on without recriminations.

The rugby club is a very hospitable host and its kindly president sometimes lays on a buffet after training. One evening staff arrived to collect Malcolm and were gobsmacked to find him handing around a china plate of steaming sausage rolls. "He has to eat alone off paper plates," they protested, "because he steals from other peoples' plates and smashes the crockery".

Jim won't talk to you about giving respect, encouraging autonomy, low arousal behaviour management, or offering and supporting choices. He simply does all these things, not because he's been trained to do them but because he sees Malcolm as his friend and a person... a person with pride and dignity, and the right to a say in his own life. A man seeking to love and be loved. Jim intuitively posed the question, "What is a good life for Malcolm?"

Discussion Points:

o   **If we accept someone's reputation without checking out its veracity we may be compounding their problems.**

- Active acceptance and hospitality often elicits reciprocal behaviour in others.
- Bizarreness breeds bizarreness.

Andrew: Putting a spin on things!

Andrew was thirteen when I first met him. By that time he had spent more than four months as an in-patient in a child psychiatry unit. He had been admitted for treatment for day and night-time enuresis and encopresis (urinary and faecal incontinence) and as a school phobic who was said to attract unmitigated bullying from his peers. Andrew came across as timid, effeminate, lacking self-confidence and abrim with self-loathing. Yet he was very sensitive to the needs of others, showed a capacity to respond in a caring way, and was possessed of excellent manners and social etiquette. His parents were also gentle and considerate people.

It seemed to me that his treatment comprised a toileting chart and attendance at the hospital school. The former seemed to be having little impact while the latter - resulting I thought from a good relationship with the school's vigorous and enthusiastic deputy head, who both taught him and provided a strong role model – had promise. Unfortunately the long summer school holiday was imminent.

Coming from a youth work and juvenile justice background – and with a personal love of outdoor pursuits, sports and all that surrounds them – coloured the way I went about my work as a young professional. And the abiding lessons I derived from these experiences – both in respect of the people served and the teams I led – have stayed with me and informed my practice later in my career. That summer was something of a challenge for the unit team, as they came to terms with the discontinuation of uniforms and the notion that we did our work wherever was necessary to get a result for each child; and for the kids, as they experienced many of the ordinary experiences of childhood from which they had been excluded by reason of their conditions. During these seven weeks I got to know all of the children quite well. And I got to know Andrew - on hikes, in youth hostel self-catering kitchens, during night-time wide games, and in boisterous kick-abouts – as a brave, resilient and talented young man. In the group of nine to fourteen-year-olds with us at that time he was one of the oldest and it was natural to ask the older kids to take more responsibility. Andrew blossomed under this regime.

And we discovered a genuine talent!

There was a table tennis table in the unit's day room. It was not used a lot until I arrived as it took up a lot of space, the children did not often ask for it, and none of the staff played. However, I did and I'd just recruited a young SEN who it transpired played in a local league, like me. Under our tutelage a number of the children showed interest and promise, but Andrew demonstrated not only talent but the ability to respond to coaching and improve with every session. During those few weeks Andrew had moved cognitively from being a helpless and hopeless victim to:

o   someone who was trusted to take a lead;

o   being encouraged to sleep in a youth hostel bunk by folk who did not think it was the end of the world if he soiled the sheets (and that included the hostel warden);

o   someone who did not 'freeze' on an abseil rope, just got on with his kayak capsize drill when asked, and overcame his fears to lead a group of younger children through the pitch darkness of a, unbeknownst to him, very carefully controlled woodland, night-time orienteering exercise;

o   a table tennis player with the skills and self-belief needed to hold their own against other talented players – with power and deft control of spin.

I surmised that it would be helpful to generalise the progress being made in Andrew's personal development. Daytime incontinence was by now a very rare event and he was beginning to experience an occasional 'dry' night in the unit. By this time he was spending his weekends at home with similar progress during the day but continued nocturnal incontinence.

So we formed a new table tennis club, comprising patients, family members and staff of the unit and we joined the local league who were delighted to accept our late entry, literally a couple of weeks before the commencement of a new season. That year we entered two teams, both playing in the bottom division, with the home fixtures fulfilled in the unit day room on a Friday evening after the residential service had closed for the weekend.

Suffice it to say that the 'A' team - comprising Andrew, Anil (the SEN), two other young patients, and me (perm three for each match) – was promoted at the end of the first season and for the next two. Andrew had a 90% average at the end of year one. By then he was travelling back on Fridays to play because he had been discharged home before Christmas and, with a little outreach help, had made a happy transition to a new school the following January. By the end of the season Andrew was not only playing competitively with us but had also joined a thriving club in his own town.

Prospects began to change for Andrew because:

o   he felt better about himself;

o   he started to take a lot more responsibility for himself;

o   he ceased to be a victim;

o   he spent time with and as an accepted member of a cross-section of the everyday community and learned from others' life experiences;

o   especially in terms of how to deal with aggression, intimidation, teasing and disappointment;

o   he belonged.

Discussion Points

o   **Andrew's story is typical of so many people I've worked with over the years. The therapeutic, treatment-oriented or 'health model' approach adopted by so many professionals seems to reflect what they/we do rather than what the person fundamentally needs.**

o   **Assessment seems to be a process of codifying needs into things that they/I do or things that other professionals do and justify referral.**

o   **We then seem to limit how we work to stuff that can be done 'efficiently' in a clinic, interview room, or, heaven forefend, on a home visit.**

o   **I would contend that we can have much more impact working with communities, with groups, attending to common and fundamental human needs, than we do by concentrating to the exclusion of all else on individuals and even families.**

o   **This is not an argument for a new profession, the rehabilitation of community work, nor additional resources. It** is a proposal that all professionals should get engaged in things that work rather than imposing their particular expertise.

o   And it is a challenge to policy makers and managers to think hard about the validity of the recording, workload management and targeting imperatives that limit professionals to what are, in my view, institutionalising and service-centric modes of practice and, inevitably, thinking.

Wye not?

People tend to have low expectations of people with learning disabilities. People who work with them and more often than not their families and friends frequently share this characteristic. People consequently see the needs of people with learning disabilities in terms of care and protection and, all too often, succeed in ensuring that neither is secured.

I had been appointed to turn around a failing service (see *Respite Care*) for children with learning disabilities and quickly appreciated that the staff team not only entertained low expectations of the children in their care, they also had a pretty poor opinion of themselves.

I had, as outlined in a previous vignette, taken quite radical steps to begin the process of agreeing a shared vision, creating a proactive leadership, building committed and can-do teams, and instilling developmental, child-centred practice. But I knew instinctively that I was selling pie in the sky to a lot of good folk who did not have the benefit of my experiences, nor my self-belief about making a difference. They, like Doubting Thomas, needed to experience, to witness, living examples of the vision I was explaining. It was not enough to visit others who could do these things. They simply did not believe that they were up to it and, as Henry Ford so aptly remarked, "Whether you believe that you can or you can't, you're right!"

I knew that, in the course of time, the strategy that was messily unfolding had a chance of delivering the outcomes I wanted. But I was by then experienced enough to know that it would be a long haul. Things happen, such as the promotion or pregnancy of key players, and put back the realisation of plans for months and sometimes irretrievably. In my guts I knew that we needed some culture changing examples, some beacon events. So I scatter-gunned some ideas and was energetic in supporting the intrapreneurs who took up the challenge.

One initiative I led myself. As a youngster I had participated in the annual 100-mile canoe 'survival' test that was usually held on the River Wye over the Whitsun weekend. In my subsequent work I had accepted the challenge with a number of groups of young clients and seen troubled youngsters grow in self-esteem and maturity as a result of their participation. On each of these occasions the event had impacted far wider than the on-the-water participants. Parents had seen their youngsters in a new light. Organising the bank crew and support functions had involved other youngsters, volunteers, family members, and strengthened my staff team.

I had re-organised the booking arrangements for residential respite care at the centre so that, as a rule, children were admitted with the same small group each time they stayed and with peers of similar age and abilities. A group of 5 teenagers who attended the same special school and knew each other well were with us every six weeks for either 3 or 4 nights. The two girls and three lads were, it seemed to me, pretty capable but used to sitting back while grown-ups did far too much for them, including decision-making. A quick look at their plans, such as they were at that time, confirmed that services seemed pre-occupied with equipping them with personal care skills and little else. A little observation confirmed that these plans were largely ignored in the rush for everyone to be ready for school transport and for less credible reasons on non-school days.

I, with the Respite Service Team Leader, convened planning discussions around a single question, "What are we trying to achieve with this young person?"

Concurrently, I asked the 5 youngsters if they would like to have a go at canoeing. I had found out that there were sessions at the local baths and suggested that I would take them if they wished. They were keen. I advised their parents in their communication books and asked that swimming gear should be packed on their next stay. One session was enough to get the buy-in of the kids. They learned their capsize drills and gained confidence in the warmth and safety of the heated pool, and by the end of lesson one had stopped going round in giggling circles and were all able to make their pretty unstable bath trainers travel in a chosen direction. The sessions were weekly and they wanted to go every week. So I contacted their families and cut a deal; if they brought the children we would supervise the sessions.

It was winter and the availability of an indoor club was a godsend. As time went on, the viability of my initial premise seemed to strengthen. Making the transition to cold, running water would be the test. During the winter a number of staff had helped with the indoor sessions and a couple had taken to kayaking like the clichéd ducks to water. The on-the-water team of my imagination was beginning to form. In April I accessed enough boats and kit through old youth service contacts and, on a drizzly Saturday morning, we 'tested the water'. In the morning we paddled a couple of miles. In the afternoon it was nearer five.

Two weeks later we were testing ourselves on the small rapids between Ross and Symonds Yat on the Wye. By then I'd shared my 'fantasy' with the 5 youngsters, the service staff, and finally the kids' parents. "If you had proposed this six months ago I would have told you that you were mad, but now..." was a common response. The families were unanimous in wanting their children to give it a go and we had lots of volunteers to help out and offers of loans of equipment, including a touring caravan with driver!

Five weeks later, over a long weekend during which we tolerated both icy winds and sunburn and were effectively dependent on borrowed kit (both boats and tents), we participated with hundreds of other young people in the 100-mile event. A bank crew of family and staff volunteers, with siblings of the youngsters on the water and three other youngsters who used the respite service, set up and dismantled each night's campsite, did the catering, and ensured sustenance for the paddlers at stopping places along the route. Three of the youngsters completed, the other two paddling more than 60 miles, and all took part in the final stretch from Monmouth to Tintern on the Bank Holiday Monday morning and joined in the massed celebrations at the finish. All of the youngsters had hurt. We all had blisters, sore muscles, stiff backs. We had all moaned and whinged. But we had all achieved and demonstrated strengths and qualities that, perhaps, we did not know we had. We had demonstrated a capacity to learn, and resilience and tenacity. As Stephen, one of the paddlers, put it, "The hardest bit was starting again in the morning – but I did!"

Most of all, the initiative caused a culture shift. For a lot of people, though not for everyone ("but my Charlie couldn't have done that", while not appreciating that it is only a matter of finding the right challenge for us all!), children with learning disabilities were redefined. They were no longer just seen as recipients of care and protection. Instead, people were more alert to their talents, their qualities, and our responsibility to find ways to maximise their potential. More than anything else the 'with disabilities' was to some extent sidelined and our youngsters' needs to be children first was not just recognised but understood. Five young people emerged from the experience with enhanced self-confidence, improved social skills and more assertive personalities.

Discussion Points:

o   **Talk is cheap. Actions speak louder than words.**

o   **In pushing the boundaries it is important to make use of our own talents. I know people who use theatre, music and dance as vehicles through which devalued people can be enabled to achieve.**

o   Projects are an essential medium for team building and culture change.

o   We are hindered and limited by both our beliefs and our self-belief. It is important to test the veracity of our assumptions and find ways around our self-limitations where this impacts upon the folk we aspire to assist.

A Brief History of *TACT*
Borocourt – 'The Silent
Minority'

In 1989 I was part of a team convened to advise West Berkshire Health Authority on the future of its services for people with, as it was then, mental handicaps subsequent upon the exposure of the conditions at Borocourt Hospital in the *World in Action* 'Silent Minority' television documentary. By the end of the year I was the Director of Services responsible for implementing the recommendations in the team's report.

I was pretty experienced in leading hospital closures, and the design and implementation of resettlement strategies, but the challenges at Borocourt were unusually daunting. While there were some strong resettlement elements in place, the operational arrangements in the group of hospitals were little changed from those that obtained when the 'scandal' had broken. The Director of Nursing Services had gone but the medical staff - whose arrogance and stubbornness, in the view of many, underpinned the failure to respond to increasingly obvious and severe shortcomings – were still in place. The nursing and care staff teams were demoralised, defensive and fearful – led by nursing officers who knew that their jobs were on the line. They were right. Within four months I had deleted 16 management units and replaced them with just 6, 3 of which were led by people recruited externally. While the nursing issues, including a ridiculous backlog of serious disciplinary matters, were resolved in months, it took much, much longer to resolve the medical staffing issues.

Meanwhile we, at least initially, had few fans amongst the families of the hospital residents who wanted us to make the unacceptable acceptable and angrily opposed our closure plans. As I met with small groups of families I was increasingly aware of their psychological dilemma. They had no reason to trust 'the authorities' who had let them and their relatives down. So they had no reason to trust us. But they also felt extremely guilty. Those who had visited were well aware of the increasingly dehumanised and deprived service. They had repeatedly reported their concerns but, fearful that they would have to take responsibility for their relatives (perhaps to the extent of taking them home), many felt that they had colluded with the hospital management and not advocated as actively as they should.

We didn't make a pretence of consulting and then disregarding what the families were telling us. I was very clear that not only was the hospital unsaveable from a financial or an estates (some parts of the premises were a major fire hazard and the heating system was in meltdown with a £6 million estimate for replacement), it was also, as a model of support for people with learning disabilities, indefensible. I tried to explain our objections to the institutional model and the improvements that they might expect from a system founded upon small group living in ordinary houses in ordinary streets. Nobody seemed to understand or, perhaps, even listen. They had come with their demands, not to debate, and they did not expect to 'win'.

In response to a, "What assurances can you give us?" question, I replied that I was clear that the closure and resettlement programme needed to be implemented quickly, that I was in no doubt that we were unlikely to get arrangements right for everybody, and that might mean the majority of people, the first time around, but that I could assure everyone that we would stay around and keep working at it until we got it right. I shuddered, thinking that I shuddered, thinking that I'd just blurted out an unhelpful 'open mouth and stick in foot' 'Malapropism'. It turned out otherwise. One of the loudest complainants let it be known that he was reassured. "For the first time in living history," he said, "I have not been offered empty promises and castles in the air". He could do business with someone who owned up to the challenges to be faced. He trusted us to do our best.

He was a leading light in the Hospital Friends organisation and the parent of a young woman with a very challenging reputation.

His opinion counted. When *TACT* was constituted he was a founder member and trustee. His interjection spurred helpful and supportive remarks from many others.

'Tell it as it is' became the rule of thumb for every meeting with all stakeholders and the beginnings of trust were established, and subsequently strengthened as actions reflected our words.

'Keep your promises' was the second non-negotiable. We made unambiguous commitments to all the Borocourt stakeholders:

o   That we would deliver the closure by March 1993 in order to ensure that the preserved rights of all the residents were honoured.

o   That - while we were convinced that taking time over the process produced no better outcomes and often allowed time for 'reactionary forces' to regroup – we saw resettlement as the beginning of a journey to a tailored and progressive support plan for each individual. We expected to get things wrong and make compromises during the closure phase but that this would not be the end of the story.

o   That ours was a long-term commitment. We would not deliver the closure and then decamp.

These commitments shaped the future.

The journey begins...

TACT was established out of necessity and was a direct consequence made to the Borocourt stakeholders, and especially the residents and their families, in 1990.

We had progressed the closure programme very quickly. The smaller hospital, Waylands, had been closed and its 105 residents resettled in little more than a year. Concurrently, we had resettled another sixty people from the most worrying areas in Borocourt and closed these wards.

All of this had been achieved without Regional Health Authority support and the local Health Authority had found additional funds. Indeed the RHA had been less that communicative, its nose out of joint following the publication of the inquiry report that had been scathing in respect of the region's inaction and lack of support for West Berkshire.

However, it would have been impossible to achieve the closure to time – and that was essential to the financing assumptions – without capital and bridging funding from the RHA. We had completed the statutory closure consultations and prepared a detailed and finely costed closure and resettlement plan that had been submitted to the region. In our timescale a week was a long time. It seemed a lifetime before we got the green light. A number of capital programmes had been deferred and the Borocourt closure had been inserted into the budget. We had £13 million to disburse flexibly in respect of capital and bridging costs. By now it was June 1991. We had 21 months to deliver the plan.

Just a few days later our enthusiasm was dashed. Under instruction from the Treasury, the Health Minister suspended the 'Merryfield Advice', a formula that enabled those of us engaged in the closure of long-stay institutions to circumvent strict Treasury rules that insisted that any given project should only receive funds from one government department. This facility was necessary as the new homes and support arising through resettlement was funded jointly from each person's benefits entitlements and the NHS.

This dispensation had been made specifically to enable the closure of isolated and isolating mental health, mental handicap, and physical disability long-stay institutions but, somewhere, the provisions had been used to close a geriatric hospital, loosing the justifiable anger of the affected local authority. On August 8th the Minister announced the cancellation of the advice with a rider that arrangements made prior to that date would remain lawful but that Health Authorities progressing institutional closures should seek legal advice. The progress of the 1991 *NHS and Community Care Act* provided a backdrop for this decision. Local Authorities were to assume lead responsibility for community care and they were not hamstrung by the Treasury Rules. That did not help us, however. The implementation date was April 1993 and nobody anticipated full implementation before 1995.

We, and the RHA, took independent advice from expert barristers. They (thankfully) came to similar conclusions. It would be unlawful for the Health Authority to implement its plans itself. But it was empowered to make grants to charitable and voluntary organisations. It would be lawful to engage such an organisation to implement the programme. It would be sensible to engage with an agency that could trade, given the likelihood of lots of property transactions, probably a friendly society or a charity with a significant trading arm.

By now it was late September and meetings were quickly convened with a number of potential partners. Nobody seemed excited by the opportunity. It felt as if many of the agencies wanted to be wooed. We were struck by the conservative and unconfident stance adopted by so many of the big voluntary agencies we approached. They felt that the timescales were unrealistic and had worries that they would be left 'holding the baby' when these 'innovative' funding arrangements were audited (the NHS had been empowered to grant aid voluntary agencies from its inception!). We soon appreciated that we were unlikely to make progress this way. We were not talking to 'can-do' organisations and many gave us the impression that they were in the presence of 'wide-boys' (and girls!). With hindsight I am certain that the deciding factor was the timescale. They did not appreciate how comprehensive our preparations were and, as we later appreciated when trying to progress creative partnerships, operated within structures that made real delegation and speedy decision-making impossible.

I was now mid-October. From the start, team members had, in frustration, been saying, "Let's do it ourselves," but had been less than certain when I had 'unpacked' the issues around leaving the public sector and the implicit professional and personal risks. However, we were making no progress, very valuable time was leaching away, and I was beginning to get worried calls from families who were aware that the programme had stalled, and the first inklings of seeds of cynicism from staff.

The next six weeks are a haze for me. Four of us – the Finance Director, Senior Clinical Psychologist, my PA and me – somehow signed up to be the founding staff of *TACT*. I volunteered our plan to the Health Authority and progressed with the planning – recruiting a management committee, appointing lawyers, finding premises, writing the rules and articles, applying for both Charity and Industrial & Provident Society status, negotiating start-up funding and the ongoing grants arrangements, agreeing a method statement and operational agreement with West Berkshire, sorting out our own contracts of employment, and a plethora of other essentials – while a decision was made. I guess that, in truth, the decision made itself. The urgency of the situation - where the financial consequences alone of not delivering the Borocourt closure to time were bad, but of not delivering at all were horrendous – linked to the maelstrom of joint activity necessary to midwife the birth of *TACT* generated an unstoppable inevitability. I do not remember a substantive decision being made but rather a series of agreements that were based upon an assumption that a decision had been made.

So on the 1st December 1991 four of us turned up for work at our new offices in Pangbourne. On that date we were registered as a charity. Three weeks later we were an Industrial & Provident (Friendly) Society. Sixteen months later Borocourt was closed and we still had not fully codified who did what between our health colleagues and ourselves. We had been constituted as an independent commissioning agency but, in the final phase of the closure, had fallen into a role as a specialist provider and, in the context of this book, this is where the *TACT* story really starts.

Becoming a Specialist Provider – Facing the Facts

Borocourt was home to a disproportionate number of people who had acquired the 'challenging behaviour' label. Around 40% of the population were deemed to need services that had the capacity to manage their behaviour in non-aversive and proactive ways and these figures were generated as a result of planning by a resettlement team that set the bar high when setting out the criteria for 'challenging'. Truth be told, Borocourt justified its 'Silent Minority' notoriety. A lot of its population had been institutionalised and brutalised in both Borocourt and other settings, such as the Smith Hospital, over decades and much of what had happened in the years leading up to our involvement had only served to reinforce the damage. Borocourt was rarely a kind place.

It was also home to the Regional Medium Secure Forensic Service; purpose built, super secure and, as far as I was concerned, a monument to the absence of a continuum of care services for intellectually disabled offenders.

We had written very demanding service specifications for some of the people with the most challenging reputations. We were looking for providers who would be kind, stimulating, person-centred, non-aversive and generally focused upon helping people 'get a life' and break the hopelessness mould that seemed to surround these people. For a while we thought we had found such a provider but the proof was in the practice and, while the initial outcomes for folk were indeed a big step up from the hospital, we found these services to be still focused on control and insular, not very interested in, let alone committed to, integrating with their local communities. Other interested parties all seemed to base their regimes upon secure accommodation and chemical controls.

Consequently, as time ticked on and the closure deadline beckoned, there were a dozen or so people without providers and the local authority was looking for similar 'solutions' for some other folk. There was talk of placing people in private special hospitals if a resolution was not found quickly. We sought to veto this and, along the way, found that we had volunteered to provide the services, as an interim solution at least. We had developed the specification so we must know how to do it?

At this point cold reality struck. I recall a planning session that started with a rhetorical statement, "The only clue we have about how to start this project is that we know all about how not to do it!" Our original service specification had been a request for detailed proposals based upon pen pictures of the people to be served, some suggested groupings, a list of desired outcomes, and an indication of the contract price. We knew some of the people quite well so set to work imagining what it would take to help them achieve the lives we had envisaged. Our recognition of the limitations implicit in our past experiences did not necessarily give rise to very innovative thought. We already knew, at least intuitively, that requiring people with bizarre and difficult behaviours to live together was not a clever idea but we, as commissioners, had become increasingly unchallenging of clumsy funding and staffing formulas that enabled accurate resource planning but were unhelpfully prescriptive and shut down person-centred creativity at the sharp (delivery) end. So we developed four group homes – 6, 5, 3 and 3 places respectively – and spent the next decade responding to unnecessary problems.

On the positive side, we espoused action research as a valid service methodology and, although the terminology had not yet emerged, our medium was person-centred planning. We had been able to list some of the criteria for a decent life supported by a kind and learning service. Now we set off on the journey to discover sustainable ways of delivering and developing our vision.

Jenna

Jenna was in her 20s and had been in NHS care for many years under the supervision of medical staff when she moved out of Borocourt. She was seen as very difficult to support; aggressive towards others and self-injuring with a severe learning disability aggravated by psychosis. She had been described as autistic. The regime around her had essentially been one of containment.

Jenna moved into a house with 2 other people, a man and a woman. The other woman shared Jenna's aggressive and unpredictable reputation. We had been daft to try to support them both progressively in the same place and we had to find another solution very quickly. The service manager was a very reflective and tenacious young woman. She, I think, had a social care background and no health-related professional training but she had bought in to our mission, saw her job as that of getting Jenna a kinder and more purposeful life, and she got to grips with getting to know her properly and, in doing so, undertook the observation and assessment process that had, so clearly, been neglected within specialist health services.

She noted her unusual 'mousey' body smell, that her urine had the same but stronger aroma, and her pale almost albino colouring. She observed the evidence of aural and visual hallucinations and monitored fits. Concurrently, she began to research and, having recognised phenylketonuria (PKU) as a possible cause, was tenacious in insisting that Jenna should be screened for the condition.

The 'good news' was that PKU was confirmed; the 'bad news' that it was far too late to do anything about it.

But, in pursuing her research, the service manager had come across accounts of significant progress being made when dietary therapy was introduced with older people. This would involve removing all high protein foods from Jenna's diet. There could be no meat or dairy products and she would need an alternative source of protein in a phenylalanine-free formula. When she investigated sources of these foods and supplements she found injunctions that they should be effectively prescribed and administered under clinical supervision. Another frustration – she believed that Anna was entitled to try the therapy but expert opinion said that it would be a fool's errand. Once again she pestered and persisted, finding a dietician who was supportive.

Suffice it to say that tenacity was still needed to improve the culinary skills of the staff team so that they were able to transform the unappetising special diet into a varied and palatable menu, and even then to get Jenna to eat it. And tenacity paid off as Jenna's mood lightened; the frequency, intensity and duration of her 'outbursts' diminished progressively and were much more attributable to circumstances, and less seemingly psychotic episodes were observed. Jenna was much calmer and engaged more frequently and for longer periods.

The reason for telling this story is not to promote the use of dietary therapy with adults with PKU. It seems to have benefited Jenna but a whole raft of other influences, not least the intensively personalised support that she had recently started to receive, could have played a part.

My, hopefully, obvious observation is that qualitative changes seem to result from people assuming personal responsibility and being given the authority to make a difference. Jenna's previous life, contained in a long-stay institutional setting with little apparent aspiration for change, was maintained by a hierarchical structure with a distant and often, in my experience, disinterested figurehead. Long-stay folk were essentially the business of clinical assistants and the occasional medic in training. Their files were frequently litanies of minor ailments and medication changes with occasional bursts of activity if clinical drug trials were being undertaken or a driven charge nurse appeared on the scene.

> People make a difference. Effective organisations support their people to make a difference.

The first couple of years were exhausting, sometimes demoralising, and comprehensively challenging. Fortunately we had not been naïve and had not expected any different. We knew that established and institutionalised patterns of behaviour – and here we were talking about ourselves, our new staff teams, and the much damaged people we were supporting – would not change overnight in response to nice environments and kind people. We were very aware that we would have our work cut out to sustain kindness.

Discussion Points:

By now you'll have noticed some recurrent themes.

o   One is my deep belief, derived from experience, that it is essentially stupid and illogical for governments and their bureaucracies/agents to imagine that they have much of a role in the 'commissioning' of new thinking, inspiration, innovation and social change. The best systems can do is nurture a culture of open-mindedness, encourage an element of no-strings funding of new ideas and be hopeful patrons.

o   However, even this is probably fanciful. For example, the agencies established to encourage social entrepreneurs – the last place that a successful entrepreneur would work – immediately set to work to identify immutable rules for would-be entrepreneurs and make compliance with their operational manual a condition for funding. Those who won't comply are excluded or offered business development consultancy to help them focus their ideas. It is astounding how many bureaucrats - who have never innovated, never been inspired, and never stuck tenaciously to an unpopular idea or cause - are permitted to claim expertise and get paid for it!

o   It seems that Lord Mawson shares my analysis. He writes, 'The learning by doing approach is the tried and tested approach of the social entrepreneur. We call into question the systems and processes of government, which are still run by well-qualified civil servants who rarely get hold of the pieces themselves and whose approach has so failed many of our poorest communities'.

- ○ **Simply put: our politicians and bureaucracies have delusions of grandeur and aspire to implement widespread change through systems and rules. But people, over-compliant as we often are, are rarely inspired or moved to their own innovations by these impositions. Social innovators usually 'get hold of the pieces', moving and enabling people, and hence eliciting the added value that derives from ownership and empowerment. The system implicitly disempowers and subtly enslaves. The innovator empowers and liberates.**
- ○ **The challenge for policy makers is to envision a world of expansive and generalised social innovation. For sure they won't be able to control it!**

It can take two to three years for people who have been subjected to control and restraint oriented 'specialist services' to really believe that we are not going to impose our will upon them and lose the compulsion to find out what it will take to make us. That's sometimes because we have to resort to a level of restraint in order to ensure peoples' safety because we weren't paying attention and missed the opportunity for other strategies – so we inadvertently break trust. It is also because it takes a long time to really get to know someone, to effectively listen to the things that really matter to them, and to envisage and start to deliver a holistic support programme that attends to those priorities.

We had all the usual teething problems of new services as we implemented our first tranche of services. We made a few bad appointments; leaders who didn't, managers who couldn't. We learned from our initial mistakes about the absolute necessity of building interdependent teams during induction and leaving people in no doubt about the values, principles, do's and don'ts of our practice. It was crucial to avoid ambiguous language. Folk who work in care services know that professional language too often speaks with a forked tongue or is open to wide interpretation. We quickly discovered, as you might logically expect, that in the absence of vibrant leadership and a constantly restated and demonstrated vision too many staff reverted to autopilot, doing what they had always done, retreating to their comfort zones.

And buried among these challenges were others, notably authority, delegation, and personal responsibilities. We had started out by appointing a Head of Services. She was a very talented, committed, hard-working, principled and determined leader. She took full responsibility for everything associated with the services she commissioned and the consequence was paralysis. Decisions were constantly deferred pending discussions with and, effectively, permissions from her. The service managers were effectively hobbled and this was counter-cultural to the learning-by-doing ethos of the rest of the leadership team. This was the inertia we had experienced throughout the care system, something we had sworn we would avoid. And its effects were truly debilitating. The Head of Services was overwhelmed and demanding a deputy and support staff – a request that I resisted – and the leadership team, that shared the on-call/out-of-hours responsibilities was going under too.

It felt, for all of us, that we were always at work; continually responding to crisis call-outs, people seeking advice, people looking to off-load, and petty requests for permissions. And we were increasingly aware that two things repeatedly hampered the progress we wanted to make:

○   Something that stopped staff doing the sensible things that, had they been done, would either have been proactively positive or, conversely, defused problematic and possibly explosive situations. Through discussions and observation we came to the conclusion that a risk averse, permission based, and increasingly punitive operational culture linked with systems that severely delimited personal responsibility were at the root of the problem. Our Head of Services argued, not incorrectly, that compliance with our contracts demanded that we functioned in this way. I asserted that our responsibilities to get decent lives for the folk we served had precedence over the statutory compliance issues. We were not only failing them, the conflict of loyalties was also putting our coalface staff at risk of both physical injury and total demoralisation as they sought to achieve our shared vision with 'both hands tied'. I asked, "How can disempowered staff be expected to empower, or create an environment for the empowerment of others, especially the most excluded and disempowered in our society?" It led to a parting of the ways and the beginning of a lot of experiments and initiatives that incrementally added up to a more effective and sympathetic way of working. It is really challenging to build and sustain a method based upon a trust and gift centred philosophy in the midst of the unthinking blame culture that characterises so much of contemporary British popular culture. But it is right to try.

o   Second, we had initially got a little carried away with our determination to deliver non-aversive and life-enhancing environments and underplayed the need for teams to be skilled in what would now be described as low arousal behaviour management. Some members of the leadership team had worked for large parts of their careers with folk with extremely challenging reputations and were very confident of their own talents. Somehow we overlooked that we wouldn't be running the services ourselves and doing the necessary modelling and on-the-job training with staff. Initially, the service managers had not the knowledge, skills, experience and confidence to do this and, while having fully bought-in to our criticisms and opposition to control and restraint based approaches, had only that background to fall back upon *in extremis*. The consequence was that we were constantly being called out to sort out crises that, had we got it right in the first place, would not have occurred. This was bad enough – a disaster for the clients involved – but made worse by the fact that we were good at fire-fighting. We accrued the ambiguous status of 'knights on shining chargers'; we were held in awe and respect because people were dependent upon us, and deeply resented for the same reason. And worse, we were reinforcing peoples' feelings of incompetence. This was, perhaps surprisingly, far easier to remedy than the 'empowerment' issue. Once again, a recurring theme, a large part of the solution arose because we made connections outside the health and social services world.

Our learning around these two challenges is outlined in the next two sections.

The Disempowered Can't Empower – Evolving a culture that encourages everyone to take responsibility, to take good risks, to fight back against the blame culture, to make good mistakes, to make a difference

I would like to start from some fairly contentious assumptions. Let's assume that most people are essentially honest, reliable, well-motivated, and want the respect, recognition and affection of others. Further to this let's consider the proposition that in any given activity of life the strongest influences upon us consist of our own internalised 'value base' and our peer group. Then add to the mix that we all search for purpose in our lives and tend to find these in our relationships, passions and vocations. This is true for me. I imagine that you are thinking, Yes, that pretty much sums things up for me, too. I would go even further and propose that the majority of people would assert that my profile assumptions also have redolence for them.

If I am right a fundamental question arises for me. Why, oh why, do our dominant employment and human management assumptions and systems operate on the basis that none of this is true? And I then answer my own question as follows:

- most employers have no interest in the self-realisation of their employees;

- most are only interested in the delivery of their job specification;

- and, in their pre-occupation with control, the elimination of the dishonest and incompetent, and the achievement of predetermined results, make their good people resentful and cynical;

- and exclude the possibility (I would assert the certainty) that corporately the good folk who comprise the large majority of their workforce will over-perform, often exponentially and with unpredicted benefits.

I had grown up in a world of farming, tradesmen, garages, pubs, hotels, local shops and small engineering workshops – small family businesses that generally employed less than a dozen people, often only a couple. These were concerns where, it seemed to me, everybody mucked in. Nothing seemed to be below the dignity of the bosses or beyond the ambition, if not the competence, of most of the workforce. People did not seem to clock watch and worked tolerantly if not always uncomplainingly around the exigencies of each other's lives. The boundaries between work and people's personal lives seemed pretty blurred and that seemed to work. There was an interdependency in these businesses that was rarely evident in big companies and public services (with the notable exception of some village schools) and an implicit recognition that success and security resided in pleasing your customers. All these businesses stood or fell according to their reputation and word of mouth mattered.

Throughout my career I had worked, primarily as a leader, in large public sector organisations and, from personal experience and observing others' initiatives, come to the conclusion that it was beyond my orbit to build, develop and deliver a strong vision and mission with and through a large number of people. My leadership style demanded regular personal contact with everyone involved and that seemed to be the case for everyone else I knew who had made a significant difference in the human services field. I estimated that I started to lose effectiveness at around 40 people. My optimum team was probably 20-25, and 8–10 on complex goals. It struck me that the team successes with which I had been involved were all characterised by one thing, I had enjoyed a lot of autonomy and extensive delegation. I had been accountable for outcomes and not required to report on process. Perhaps it went with the territory? I had built my career as a trouble-shooter, as someone prepared to take on and find solutions for intractable problems. As my reputation had grown I had taken on tougher challenges and been accorded wider autonomies in order that creative solutions might be found. In these circumstances my bosses tended to be my servants rather than my overseers. They helped me negotiate unhelpful bureaucracies, access needed resources, circumvent obstructions, and opened doors that might have otherwise stayed barred to me.

It seemed to me - though hardly as cerebrally as I am recording it here, much of what I did was intuitive, suck it and see stuff - that the first big step must be to effect full delegation to service manager – extensive authority and matching accountability. And the starting point here was to be recruiting and appointing people who were genuinely up for the challenge, attending effectively to their professional and personal development, and giving them the right, coaching and mentoring, sort of support. I was signed up to the principle that small is beautiful.

I won't pretend the development of a highly delegated, mission driven, and self-actualising organisation was either simple or easy. Just as disabled people who have been brutalised take a long time to come to trust, workers with long experience of line management or deferring up and working out where the line is so that they can toe it don't take easily to being trusted. To begin with they often think it's a management strategy to shift responsibility! Of course it is. It is a deal that says you have full authority to assume personal responsibility up to your level of competence. None of us know or are good at everything and most areas of our work are best progressed with others. Your boss is responsible for helping you grow your areas of competence and facilitating your work. You have authority to make judgements, be responsive to circumstances, take considered risks, and make a difference. From time to time you will get things wrong – people who do things do – and the deal is that, when mistakes happen, you do not try to cover things up and shift 'the blame'. Instead you take personal responsibility for remedying the situation. If you need help you should ask for it but only rarely will you ask someone else to assume responsibility. Trial and error, learning from what works consistently and what does not is dependent upon making 'good mistakes', mistakes that we learn from. The basis of this organisation's trust in you is your integrity. If we doubt your integrity we won't employ you.

We started with a programme for service managers and that exploration still continues in the organisation development work I do with provider agencies that continue to struggle with marrying contract compliance and commercial viability to person-centredness and encouraging risk-taking. Service (registered) managers are often in an invidious situation. They have to deal with day-to-day interactions with commissioners and regulators and sell the messiness and unpredictability of the person-centred approach to people who are sometimes operating outside their comfort zone, led by the documentation, and dependent upon the manager's compliance. Service managers have often come up through the ranks and feel subordinate to the representatives of commissioners and regulator. They are, in fact, knowledgeable and competent but much less confident and assertive. Position power and implicit coercion are an unfortunate hangover from our hierarchical past.

Hence, getting it right for and with service managers proved to be vital as otherwise they would be found out as 'trying to serve two masters' – us and our person-centred corporate goals and the funders and regulators who took a world view in conflict with our own; neither comfortable for them nor helpful for their confused teams. I quickly realised that service managers are the keystone of an effectively operating organisation.

Leadership Matters: Small is Functional

It seems to me that the basic currencies of social care commissioning and compliance monitoring, and the first resort of the media and politicians when things are said to be not as they should be, are policies and procedures. I understand the logic. They set out what is to be delivered and the organisational parameters within which the delivery will occur. I have seen tendering processes where upwards of 30 policies, with associated procedures, have been required. Most of these reflect required compliances with an ever-growing swatch of legislation and regulations. Lots of provider organisations devote a great deal of management time and resources to staying abreast with these demands, and preparing and regularly reviewing them, and in retraining staff where necessary.

The consequence is, as I see it, a skewing of weighting or priority in favour of measurable generalised compliances and away from soft or qualitative issues, and leadership in particular. I have come across lots of organisations – statutory, voluntary and private – that can boast exemplary policies and inspiring aspirations but continue to provide isolating, risk-averse and

166

stagnant services. It might be said that they comply with everything but somehow overlook the people served. This is the default position in social care and generally it is deemed acceptable. Throughout my career I have been responsible for services that, lacking inspiring leadership, have reverted to 'default'.

If you are not conversant with Ricardo Semler's *Maverick!*, the book would be a useful addition to your library. In it he recounts the occasion, early in his struggle to turn around the failing family business he had 'inherited', when he secretly toured his factory and 'vacuumed up' every copy of the business's policy manuals. He then issued spoof amendments to policies and raised them at both Board and department head meetings where they were nodded through without discussion. Clearly no-one had read, let alone thought, about them. I tried a similar stunt in the NHS with similar results. It seems to me that the myth of the power of policies needs to be exposed.

It is people, not policies, that really make a difference; and people are as powerful as their personal span of influence permits.

Having spent more than three decades seeking to achieve and sustain the delivery of supports that make a real difference in peoples' lives I am convinced that the fundamental currency of social care services is leadership. John Adair's definition of the activities of leadership very much accords with my experience:

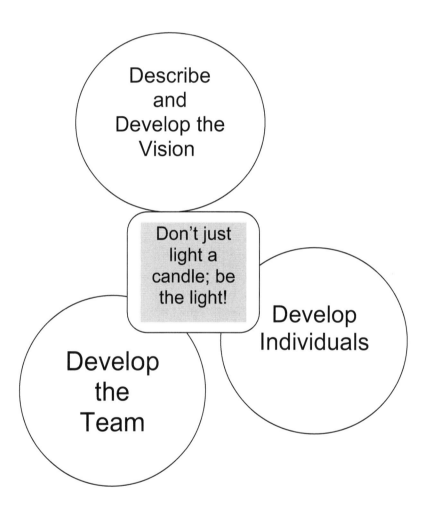

My addition, as you can see, to Adair's very helpful description – it reminds all leaders about the things we have to attend to – is a statement of the 'bleedin' obvious'. Leadership is not simply about attending to tasks. It is also about personality, relationships, insight, sometimes charisma, and usually involves integrity and being trusted. It is often about enabling others to see a way forward and proposing achievable ways of getting there. It is often about a reflective capacity or incisive focus that gives rise to clarity or tough and sometimes destabilising questions. It is often found in people who have a bit of the 'contrarian', the rule-breaker, the innovator, the driven and, hence, the hard to manage about them – but certainly not always. But they are people who march to the beat of their own drum, with their metronome being much attuned to the agendas that they are attending to – and these tend to be very focused upon the folk in their care; clients and staff. Most are not 'larger than life', colourful, nor extravert. Some don't seem to say a lot. Most have a hospitable and respectful approach to life. All model the 'spark' that they expect of others. Their integrity resides in many things but most of all in their commitment to translate words into actions; and to keep their word. It is concerned with inspiration and illumination. It is about, 'being the light'.

I have been fortunate in getting to know, and being challenged and inspired by, many leaders and innovators during my career (people who have brought about a real and lasting difference in others' lives) and, despite very different personas, they have all developed people and built functional and passionate teams around values-based visions.

So, in recognising the centrality of service managers to our mission, and in deciding that we really needed service *leaders*, it is clear, with hindsight, that a fundamental organisational revolution was under way. As I had worked on organisational restructuring at Borocourt I had been assisted by a small management and training consultancy called *Pi Associates*. We had worked very closely together and built empathy and trust so it was natural that I would turn to them to help me recruit, train and sustain my team of inspirational leaders. With their help, and in discussion with lots of insightful people within and outside the organisation, I started to clarify the leadership outcomes I wanted. Our leaders would:

o   have robust person-centred and life affirming values and walk their talk;

o   be knowledgeable, skilled, resourceful and confident in hands-on work with people with very challenging reputations - be focused, detailed, person-centred practitioners;

o   acquire 'helicopter vision' − the capacity to stand back and take a strategic and tactical view;

o   be committed to developing competence and autonomy in the members of their teams – both intellectually and emotionally at ease with creating conditions for the empowerment of others. My starting position was something akin to, 'I can't hope to achieve my goals unless I trust you with my reputation. And you cannot achieve yours unless you trust the people in your team with your reputation.'

o   be excellent organisers and project managers;

o   be fallible, and take personal responsibility for remedying failings and mistakes;

o   develop as knowledgeable and efficient administrators, doing and delegating as efficiently as possible in order that 'management' did not avoidably delimit their scope to do the real job;

o   become skilled coaches;

o   and facilitators of experimentation and problem solving (this was later redefined as effective and creative thinkers);

o   work in and as part of the community and make the most of its resources.

It seemed to me that the organisation had some of the characteristics of a pyramid sales outfit; except that our pyramid was inverted. My team comprised my few HQ colleagues – Resources Director, Director of Quality, and Development

Director at that time – and the Service Managers (at that stage around a dozen). It was my job to describe and develop the vision, to develop individuals, and to build and sustain a winning team. I had not at that stage conceptualised the arrangement as servant leadership – that construct was fed back to me by a new colleague some time later. However, just as training and, if you are sensible, it's co-produced design, is fundamental to player and team development in a rugby club (or, I guess, any other team sport) it is similarly crucial to the formation of effective social care teams. Over the years I have learned a lot about leadership from sport, both as a player but more so as a coach. Often, when wrestling with something intractable, I resort to my store of sporting experiences. The experience I will now relate had a real bearing on how I envisaged the realisation of an evolving and learning culture in *TACT*.

Abingdon RFC Under 15s - Coaching, Leadership and Enablement

In another of my passions, I had derived considerable enjoyment and success from developing talented young rugby players and building inventive and exciting teams. I had been part of the development of the mini and junior sections of the Abingdon club. My own children were players and I had coached there since they were very young. It was a comparatively small club with a limited catchment area and in the junior age groups, as 'adolescence, beer and girls' took precedence, it was often a struggle to maintain a viable team.

The squad had only 20 players. Physically it was a small team. We had a South West Division squad member and county backs but could not compete at set pieces and had learned to play off 'scraps'. In the 15-man game we could beat 'ordinary' teams but could not compete with clubs with big, well organised packs. The team was frustrated and I feared that it would not be long before players drifted away, either to the bigger clubs or other interests. Every year there was a county 7s tournament – viewed by many as the annual championships. The team had done relatively well in previous years – trading on the 'twitch' and cleverness of the backs. But each year the team lost out in the latter stages, unable to match the physicality and stamina of their opponents.

I thought that the lads could win the tournament but only if they equipped themselves to do so. They would need to be much fitter with proven stamina and we would need to develop a more disciplined style of play so that we had the ball for longer and were not so dependent upon our opponents' mistakes.

I described my vision to the squad at the first training session of the new season. Preparing for and winning the 7s tournament would be our priority. Building stamina would involve weekly cardio-respiratory gym sessions under the supervision of a fitness trainer. And training sessions would also be physically exhausting, focusing primarily on support play, ball retention and open-field tackling. I told them that this was an all or nothing proposal. It was for the team as a whole to commit to or reject the idea. If they committed they would owe it to each other to see it through.

They talked it through. Paying for the gym sessions was a problem for some; belief that the effort would pay off an issue for others. The captain, appointed by the players and a born leader, was very influential on the latter point. "Self belief is half the battle," he said. "We always score. We just need to work on scoring more than the other team."

I agreed to ask the club to subsidise the gym and found that those
who ask often get. The squad signed up to the vision and, in arriving at their commitment, had announced their intention to win the county tournament to family and friends and, especially, to the club that had agreed to back their endeavours. In my experience we are far more likely to commit fully to our goals when we have made ourselves accountable to others.

Eight months of hard graft ensued. Bodies toughened and so did minds. A team identity evolved and matured. We did not need to like each other to reciprocate loyalty and respect. Effort and improvement were celebrated. Players did not compete amongst themselves. They knew who was most naturally gifted when it came to bleep tests – they just wanted all their mates to improve on last time.

The day of the tournament came. They lost their first pool game by the odd try but instead of crumbling they learned and won their other pool games by big margins. Qualifying second in their pool they strolled through their quarter final to find themselves drawn against Bicester, the team that had narrowly beaten them earlier in the day. Steve, the captain, convened a team meeting. He took charge. "We lost earlier," he said, "because we always lose to Bicester. We were the better team but we lost it in our heads. We are fitter than they are and if we play to our plan we'll win." Dan chimed in. An unusual mix of pace, strength and elusiveness, he combined try scoring with last ditch, try-preventing tackling. "Given space there is nobody in the Bicester team who can get near me! We need to commit them to rucks and draw them in." The game plan was amended. Dan scored three tries and made two and the game was won comfortably.

The final against a Henley team made up of county players, a team that Abingdon never beat, was a close affair played over 10 minutes each way rather that the 7 of previous rounds. After conceding an early try Abingdon scored three in quick succession and then two more immediately after half time. Then Henley scored, and quickly afterwards another. It seemed that Abingdon's stamina was sapped and discipline forgotten. The leaders in the team gathered whilst a conversion was attempted and the message went out, "We keep the ball". Ball retention had been a big part of the year's training. There were three minutes to go and Henley barely touched the ball. When they did they scored. But Abingdon held on to receive the cup from a young Simon Shaw.

At the time this was as clear cut and demonstrable an example of leadership in practise as I had come across. It is an object lesson in so many of the elements of what leadership entails. I was just one of the leaders. A key element of my role was the development and empowerment of far more effective leaders than me. Having offered up a 'vision' and secured buy-in, I offered technical assistance in identifying the competences that players needed, suggesting appropriate tactics, and training sessions that I could arrange through others or deliver myself. I also offered, on a good day, moral support, belief, enthusiasm and encouragement. But I would not be on the pitch, make creative or difficult decisions for people, nor could I deliver large attendances at often painful training sessions.

Leaders emerged throughout the piece. We ended up with a team replete with leaders. Some were talented in reviving flagging morale and self-belief. Others instilled discipline, while others solved problems and introduced tactics and 'wrinkles' that made the team more competitive. Two or three, including the captain, emerged as effective decision makers. On the day of the victory I could have intervened on occasions but, I think, had the good sense, having ensured that they had acquired the necessary mental and physical competences, to let them express themselves. That took a little courage. As leaders we tend to bask in the approbation of others and like to be seen to be leading. We also worry that we need to be seen to be doing and may be criticised if goals are not realised for our apparent inactivity. Servant leadership implies not a little self-control and self-denial. Perversely, as some may experience it, the practice of empowering leadership entails taking the brickbats when things do not work out but encouraging others to take the plaudits when things go well. This seems to be counter-cultural to the competitive, self-centred and self-justifying mores of our society but, antithetically, constitutes an absolutely essential change in the behaviour of leaders if a more life affirming culture is to evolve.

Please note that the protagonists in this true story are 14 and 15-year-olds. The prevailing hegemony is, in my analysis and experience, founded upon false beliefs that:

o   associate effectiveness with qualifications and time served;

- o   (and compliance with the wishes and world view of those in charge)
- o   assume the laziness, unreliability, irresponsibility, and incompetence of people in general
- o   are elitist
- o   fail to recognise peoples' fundamental need for autonomy and self-realisation;
- o   and, in denying that need, sabotage performance.

In the *TACT* context, I had agreed and listed the attributes we needed in our leaders with the protagonists. They seemed much more relevant and person-focused than those required of a 'qualified' registered manager. An example of NVQ approach is shown on **page 85**. Unsurprisingly this competency based approach is focused upon ensuring that minimum standards are met in the care industry. My expectations of Registered Managers were far more concerned with equipping people to deliver support in a truly individualising, progressive and aspirational way. There was little option other than to support people to obtain level 4 recognition – there were recognition and compliance issues at stake and, in recognition of the diversity of service models, the NVQ model does offer considerable flexibility. However, it was necessary to provide the complementary 'core programme' shown on **page 86**.

Curriculum Example for Competence Based Assessment

Registered Manager Award NVQ Level 4   **Duration:** Approx. 1 year

Four mandatory units:

Develop, maintain and evaluate systems and structures to promote the rights, responsibilities and diversity of people
Manage a service, which meets the best possible outcomes for the individual
Manage the use of financial resources
Manage the performance of teams and individuals

Six Optional Units

Manage Activities (choose 1)

Manage activities to meet requirements
Contribute to improvements at work
Develop programmes, projects and plans
Contribute to the provision of effective physical, social and emotional environments for group care
Ensure individuals and groups are supported appropriately when experiencing significant life events
Promote the interests of client groups in the community

Manage People and other Resources (choose 1)

Take responsibility for your business performance and the continuing development of self and others
Develop teams and individuals to enhance performance
Create, maintain and develop an effective working environment
Select personnel for activities
Develop and sustain arrangement for joint working between workers and agencies
Develop your plans for the business

Manage Information (choose 1)

Provide information to support decision making
Facilitate meetings

Manage Quality (choose 1)

Manage continuous quality improvement
Monitor compliance with quality systems

Plus another two units from any of the remaining units listed above

Service Manager Leadership Programme

Foundations:

o   Explore and come to an understanding of ordinary life principles, personalisation/individualisation, loneliness and isolation, social inclusion, and citizenship from the perspectives of people who are dependent upon support. Be part of the development of the organisation's mission and vision. *In-house including user-led sessions + visiting 'inspirers'*

o   Critically explore contemporary 'best practice' in the delivery of life enhancing ordinary living support. *Visits, films, speakers, reflection/analysis and sharing of our own good things*

o   Understand and be competent in the 5 basic roles and skills of Leadership – see my leadership workshop programme for NSF. *In-house with input from Pi* Associates

o   Develop and demonstrate enhanced knowledge and skills, and operational confidence and poise, in (what became known as) low arousal and life affirming work with people with very challenging reputations. *In-house with sessions from a number of specialist agencies, Studio 3 and TSI specialists, SPACES, emerging as the most in tune with our culture and approach. Backed by focused supervision, coaching and mentoring.*

o Develop management and administration competences that facilitate the realisation of your mission and do not supplant it. *This was the brief that I gave to Pi Associates. They applied their minds to developing an on-going programme that focused on these roles in a dynamic individual and team development context. Delegation, time-management, creative financial and personnel management, and report writing were some of the core elements. We challenged ourselves to keep the organisation's essential machinery as simple, user-friendly, and 'essential' as possible.*

Further Development:

o Develop person-centred and service outcome focused strategic thinking and planning capabilities. *In-house with inspiring visitors*

o Acquire and develop problem solving competences; develop resourcefulness and creativity. *We had lots of false starts and disappointments before finding (then Career Strategies) Go MAD Thinking who helped us redefine this as a very achievable, 'become a more effective and creative thinker'.*

o Acquire and practise high tariff coaching abilities. *We started off by buying-in well thought of support and*

> *supervision training, often at significant costs. It seemed that the whole issue of oversight conflicted, in practice, with the concept of personal responsibility and development. Too often the supervisor ends up as the person accountable! The coaching element of Go MAD Thinking resolved a lot of our difficulties*

o Become expert in facilitating community inclusion, assisting people to pursue contributing and valued roles and enabling their acquisition of sustainable relationships. *We worked hard at this with lots of helpful partners, especially ADEPT, but with limited success until John McKnight opened our eyes and suggested a better strategy.*

If you compare the two programmes the differences of emphasis are unmistakable. The NVQ seems to be the outcome of a co-operation or accommodation between a businessman and a regulator. Apart from one mandatory element - concerned with managing a service which meets the best *possible* outcomes for the individual – the content is nearly all focused at groups, administration, business skills and regulatory compliance. Clients are not terribly evident as the reason for the activity. The use of the qualifying term *possible* implies recognition of limitations but probably will not address those that may be implicit to the model and alternatives. The curriculum is no doubt totally right if the desired outcome is the operation of a regulation compliant business. For me, however, the regulations do not add up to a guarantee for a decent life. Compliant services often don't get near to achieving that outcome.

By comparison, our programme was fully focused upon finding ways of equipping our service managers to deliver very tailored and progressive life outcomes for and with the people we were paid to assist. We found that, in the main, teams that are successful in their goals are much less troublesome to manage. However, this is not always true when it comes to commissioners and regulators who, too frequently (despite the protestations of their bosses), are far more concerned about the paper than the people or real quality.

Small Matters

It is not possible to locate the finalisation of 'a programme' precisely at a specific point in time. It was an iterative progress that began when we were providing just a handful of services and achieved a more stable form some 5 or 6 years later, by which time we were supporting more than 100 people and 'my team' of leaders probably exceeded 20 people. With hindsight I am in no doubt that by that time 'my team' had become too large for me to sustain the optimum leadership role that I have sought to describe. Indeed the approach which I think is functional to the achievement of a genuinely empowering organisation, lost potency when my span of control or, more properly, influence reached a dozen or so.

We responded, seemingly logically, by developing another management tier. I resisted the temptation to do this for quite a long time because my organisational experience told me that it wouldn't be long before the people reporting to me would be promulgating their own need for infrastructure and, it seemed to me, line management would inevitably both dumb down the message and undo any notion of servant management.

It would be fair to assert that the market won. Organisational machismo was regularly transfused by the foaming scarlet blood of newly won contracts. Our laudable aspiration to make progress with the individuals we supported and to demonstrate this by reduced support costs gave rise to a business strategy based upon unending growth. This was reinforced by a growing awareness that the many purchasing authorities who chose to re-tender contracts as a matter of course were often neither influenced by the best interests of the folk served nor the quality of the service provided by the *in situ* provider. An unethical marketplace encouraged promiscuous and opportunistic bidding. Lots of commissioners were seeking 'efficiency' by seeking to engage with just a small number of mega-providers and small outfits were being encouraged to merge. Organisations like *ACEVO* who should have known better, but were lead by ex-civil servants, bureaucrats, and the leaders of large charitable players, joined and even led the chorus.

So I rationalised, briefly, that by leading 'my team' inspirationally we could build upon the progress we had made. Of course, it was not long before 'my team' became an operational director's team; my new team being the HQ people with none of us having day-to-day connection with the coalface. In the context of human services, I am absolutely convinced that truly personalised, problem-solving, inspirational, empathetic, empowering and progressive practice is just about always the product of fully autonomous, intuitive and passionate servant leadership. The optimum sized organisation probably serves no more than 60 people and employs less than a dozen coalface service leaders. The organisation's boss will know everyone, customer and staff. The boss will be a very intentional and skilled servant leader – good at describing and developing the organisation's vision and mission, building a leadership team and developing individual leaders.

I knew all too well that *TACT* had grown too large and lost its agility. So I set about breaking the organisation up into autonomous, locally governed and accountable, led rather than administered, small businesses. I had been naïve. I had given a good two years notice of my intention to retire while the preparation for devolution (as it became known) was progressing. The Board had been aware of my long term intentions for much longer than that and the Chair had been actively engaged in 'strengthening the Board' in preparation for a new era. My notion of 'strengthening' had been the development of a lot stronger user and stakeholder voice alongside more business skills. To this end we had started to introduce social accounting at a divisional level and to relate this to real representation on divisional management boards.

I was soon at odds with the new Board who had not joined up to preside over their own reducing role and power and who were separated from the now established culture of empowerment and servant leadership by an unbridgeable chasm of their own control and command conditioning. I had recruited and developed servant leaders to lead and develop person-centred and community-facing and inter-relating small businesses. Within 2 years of my retirement they had all gone; all having felt that they were the victims of a new management culture that had no empathy with the humanity of disabled people, no appreciation of service users' rights to self-direction, nor belief in their talents and capacity to contribute. They seemed to believe that governance was about doing what they had always done and not about responding to the privilege of truly representing the real stakeholders in the business. I cannot blame them. The social care mainstream behaves little differently from the business world from which they came.

As a key player in this story I accept that my truth is mine alone. However, I would assert one 'absolute'. There is a relationship between the size of social care organisations; the numbers of management or, as I would have it, leadership tiers; and organisations' potential to realise their stated missions. The more tiers, the more the message is diluted, and the less likely it is that the executive leaders who should be describing and co-producing the development of the vision have meaningful interactions with either end users or service deliverers.

As a rider to this I would further observe that, as received communication, the language used to describe the values and objectives of social care within the service world is, at best, unrigorous. People who have been engaged in the field for any length of time know in their guts that there is usually a degree of sophistry in the way in which aspirational terms like *person-centred*, *self-direction*, *autonomy*, and *an ordinary life* are used. At best they have become a code or a jargon, which is exactly the way the terminology is viewed by many lay people. My approach to leadership insists that we use language as simply and accurately as possible. Of course, accuracy sometimes implies the use of precise and somewhat obscure language. This means that social care leaders engage with their teams in drilling down into **what** the achievable outcomes of their stated vision might or should be and in exploring **how** the outcomes will be delivered; and then restating the vision in real descriptions of what is to be done and the hows, whos, and wheres implicit. In addressing these issues many of the obstructions – be they attitudes and beliefs, needs for competences or resources, or matters of morale – are likely to be addressed. Most importantly, teams know that the buzz words being used have meanings that relate to those given in the dictionary and that they are not working for an equivocal organisation.

The Ability to Make a Difference – serving the customer before the regulator

Empowerment without enablement is likely to both be and be perceived as empty and tokenistic. As my young rugby players' story showed so graphically, it is one thing to know what to do and quite another to know how to do it. The training that they had received had been fit for purpose. The training that *TACT's* service leaders received was similarly fit for purpose. Our mission was to help people who had intellectual disabilities, and had come to us burdened by fearful behavioural reputations, to achieve happy, contributing, ordinary lives. We had concurrently identified three key competences for the members of their teams that were again focused upon achieving our organisation vision.

The key competences were to:

o   have a real practical grasp of person-centred practice and the values and principles that underpin this;

o   be confident in their application of the key principles of non-aversive behavioural approaches, and able to contribute to team strategies for helping individuals;

o   and be a competent problem solver, an effective thinker.

It was not 'rocket science' to come up with this curriculum. All of our staff worked with 'difficult' people. Many were lone workers for all or a large part of their time. From induction onwards, through supervision and training, we immersed our staff in a culture that insisted that the only way in which our clients were going to leave long established behaviours and reputations behind would be by being alert to their gifts and skilled in facilitating 'normal' socialisation by enabling folk to learn from and model upon the norms and behaviours of the ordinary world. It is a challenging and professional job for intelligent, gentle, resourceful and tenacious people. There is no professional recognition of its practitioners. The professions in the field tend not to get hands-on too often, arguing that their rare and valuable skills are most effectively employed in assessment, care planning and supervision. The support workers who do the hands-on job usually enjoy the same pay and status as other coalface workers. Commissioners of services can rarely be persuaded that any premium should be paid in order that skilled support workers can be rewarded for their expertise and, in my opinion, reveal a degree of probably hardly-conscious cynicism and prejudice. Implicitly they appear to believe that you cannot change people who have very challenging labels. Mostly, their assumptions around the costs of services for such people are founded upon ideas about the numbers of people that will be required to 'guard' them. The same belief system seems, from my experience, to be hard-wired into most regulators who are very interested in seeing training records for food hygiene, health and safety, and lifting and handling training but seem less interested in staff's competence to do the fundamental job.

Perhaps the human services sphere should disavow the policing of compliance with generalised standards and instead get competent to evaluate service providers' performance against their stated goals in the light of the performance outcomes agreed with their funders. This will be all the more important as more and more of the funders are individuals. If I was buying a service for myself I think I would be just as interested in the quality of menu and food as the kitchen's assumed compliance with food safety regulations. And if I have a hard- to-meet specific need, in the provider's ability to respond in an as effective and life-enhancing way as possible more intensely than in the state of their health and safety policies.

Alternatively, could we do away with the regulators altogether and redirect the funding to local non-statutory, user-led and accountable service evaluation organisations and, utilising IT for bottom-up purposes, a customer/advocate fed evaluation/scoring system similar to that applied by Amazon to collect customers' views on products and suppliers?

It was a simple fact that many of *TACT's* coalface support staff became far more knowledgeable and competent than the qualified and hugely better paid professionals, who also enjoyed significant career progression opportunities, who dropped by occasionally. I pointed this out to David Blunkett when he was, *inter alia*, responsible for vocational and employment related training. I suggested that there was an unfairness implicit in recognising nurses (I am one after all!) as graduate professionals (and in the process placing the foundation tasks of good nursing below their dignity) and not offering a similar career pathway in social care and in the process reinforcing the fallacy that social care is neither intellectually challenging nor a professional role. It seemed to me that this is itself a self-fulfilling prophecy linked to a failure to understand the habilitative and rehabilitative potential of proactive 'care'.

I suspect that the general understanding of caring and supporting persists as one of doing for and to the helpless and hapless!

Mr Blunkett's response to my question was that it simply could not be afforded. I had no reply to my further proposal that, by developing supporters who were skilled in enabling people to be less dependent and in benefit of other natural supports, we might simply use the existing resources better and serve people more effectively.

Years on, I continue to spend a lot of my time in services and, in this context worryingly, in social services/adult social care departments where it seems that less and less of the continuing professional and occupational in-service education provided is concerned with personal and professional development. Instead there seems to be an inexorable momentum towards defining training in terms of knowledge of and compliance with policies, procedures, correct use of centralised systems, and regulations. The cultural implications of this emphasis, linked as it so often is to organisational systems that reserve decision making authorities to senior managers, is to say, "Don't think for yourself, be creative, or get above yourself. You'd be a mug to take personal responsibility. You are just a representative of the system. Inure yourself to the pain and frustration of others. The relationship skills you learned when you trained might be helpful in keeping you sane!"

It was our sustained experience that empowered and enabled 'non-professional' support staff repeatedly delivered inspiring work and outcomes. Perhaps that can only happen when the leaders are prepared to trust their reputations to the best offices of their staff? And perhaps that can only happen when the leaders derive confidence from knowing the staff really well, knowing that they have equipped them with the attitudes, beliefs, knowledge and skills necessary to justify their trust, and also know about the work they are doing? But, maybe, it will be hard to sell the notion that social care organisations should be small and 'immediate' to those who derive big incomes and status from their top jobs in mega businesses?

Safe and Proactive

Before I got into my quite lengthy digression on leadership you may recall that I had mentioned our early naïvety in not equipping our teams to manage violent, aggressive and destructive behaviours confidently in non-aversive, defusing and diverting ways. Later in the piece I rediscovered Andy McDonnell and the *Studio 3* organisation he had established since we had been colleagues a decade before. But in the early days of *TACT* (as a provider) we knew of no individual or agency that was working in behavioural management from the life enhancing and optimistic perspective that we espoused.

Unsurprisingly, with hindsight, it would take most of the folk we were helping quite a long time to learn to trust us and relax into some certainty that chemical and physical 'coshes' were not part of our method. As a consequence there were lots of incidents and quite a spate of staff injuries. We were collecting quite a pile of accident and incident reports, staff morale and belief in our vision were taking a hit, and the escalation in events and their intensity was doing little to augur our desired organisational culture.

As usual we set about problem solving – thinking laterally. My children were members of a karate club. Their 3rd Dan *sensei*, Mike Prior, ran a first class operation – caring and disciplined, hard-working and fun, demanding and inclusive, competitive and nurturing, founded upon respect and hospitality. My kids loved it and so did their friends. I had got involved with the club, organising summer camps and helping out at competitions, and had got to know Mike quite well. I learned that he was employed as a trainer by quite a number of organisations, including the Department of Social Security, where front line staff were felt to be vulnerable to assaults. His job was essentially to reduce the possibility that assaults would occur but, if they did, to try to enable staff members to escape unhurt. I asked him about the content of his courses. He told me that, in a nutshell, he taught defusing and de-escalation techniques and, if all else failed (he laughed), hit and run escape skills. I told him my problem and asked him how he would help my staff and clients stay safe? "There are non-negotiables," I said. "No pain can be inflicted and restraint is an undesirable consequence, a very last resort."

I expected Mike to tell me that I must be joking but instead he asked if he might spend some time hanging about in the 'services'. I arranged this and in due course received a proposal for a training course linked to a methodology based upon what I would now describe as low arousal principles. Mike's background, outside martial arts, was in aero engineering in the

RAF. Yet he had come up with a comprehensive and graduated method based upon a whole range of 'professional' concepts from my world. He started off by stressing the importance of attending to our own behaviour and its impact on others. Then being alert to the behaviours of the person being supported, to identifying destabilising influences, and environmental and room management, of graduated options for redirecting or defusing intensifying problem behaviours and, eventually, calming physical contact progressing if necessary to safe and essentially non-bullying methods of restraint. Mike and I developed a training course and piloted it with staff working in our most challenging settings. The outcomes were remarkable, immediate and sustained. The numbers of serious incidents reported fell off steeply. Out of hours summonses for assistance became a rarity. It was clear that staff had acquired both confidence and competence. Walking the boards I concluded that, in understanding how their behaviour had a major impact upon the people they supported, our support teams had been empowered, that is enabled to genuinely take responsibility for not provoking incidents and equipped to have both options for stabilising, de-escalating or defusing situations that were getting out of hand and, crucially, safety.

We rolled the training out across all of our activities with similar impact and were working on how to sustain the improvements through induction and refresher training when Mike tragically died. In a sense Mike is an icon, a glowing example of the knowledge, skills, inventiveness and integrity that the social care world (or governmental machinery) either ignores and excludes or seeks to annexe and regulate. He was probably the most accomplished youth worker I've met in a long career, a consummate organiser, and radiated hospitality and integrity. In due course we built a relationship with *Studio 3* as our advisers and trainers in this area of work. Their leadership comprises psychologists and counsellors who know each other through judo. A coincidence?

Valuing People!

The road to *LivesthroughFriends* was characterised by a growing discomfort, a gnawing awareness that I was part of a system that is terribly good at sounding plausible about the individuality, citizenship and inherent human value of marginalised people but, in fact, much more influenced by the interests of individuals and organisations that were driven by far more pressing agendas and self-interests. In conversations with the leaders of other organisations - particularly the big, well-established and often most politically influential ones – I was aware of a gentle cynicism about the viability of a business model that helped people be less dependent on services and therefore sources of reducing income. There was almost a cartel mentality in terms of common approaches to the annual pay and prices uplift negotiations. I was increasingly struck by the perversity of the status and rewards structure. People were getting increasingly well rewarded for managing, administering, planning and commissioning 'services' while the people who actually delivered the services experienced low status, poor pay and conditions, low public trust reinforced by constant initiatives for their regulation and immersion in more and more statutory training focused upon minimum standards, no obvious career path, and their supervisors were ever more tied to the delivery of administrative compliance.

I had learned early in the *TACT* experiment that we needed staff who felt valued and empowered if we were to secure the inclusion and socialisation of our most damaged and excluded clients in a sustained way. We enjoyed some success in this as a result of our leadership approach. We were able to reward our people in terms of trust, autonomy, personal and professional development, and job satisfaction but rarely via their terms and conditions. The job satisfaction benefits largely resulted from the ways in which we invested in relevant training and interpreted and defended our approach to commissioners and regulators; the latter being too often a diversion from more productive activities.

The Essence of Leadership

Everyone, in my conceptualisation of *TACT*, was a leader from time to time and a follower at others. However, in one of those delightful paradoxes that describe the human experience, it was clear that this culture could only obtain through a cadre of top leaders who embodied servant leadership and that human spark that exposed their passions, gifts and fallibilities, while also possessing a ruthlessness and decisiveness linked to an absolute loyalty to the best interests of people we served. It is a tough discipline; melding nurturing and trust, inspiring and energising, challenging and encouraging experimentation, flak catching and coaching, with decisive 'surgery' when trust is broken, values disregarded, momentum lost or, most importantly, people abused.

Over a long career in work with people you learn that 'shit happens' in all circumstances and has to be dealt with. Over time I've developed a clear understanding that agencies that focus upon systematically addressing their deficiencies deliver inferior outcomes to those that major on maximising their gifts and illuminating their vision. I've a niggling belief that if all the intellectual effort and resources that have been devoted over the decades to 'safeguarding' children in the aftermath of iconic child abuse scandals had been made available to local communities for grassroots initiatives that promote interdependence, child welfare, parenting, community cohesion and family life, our society would be a better place. The scandals will still surface, maybe less often, but more kids will benefit and, perhaps, have better chance of growing up to be good parents.

This highlights the dilemma and challenge of the sort of virtuoso leadership that facilitates a community of leaders. It succeeds in being both the midwife and the executioner. When 'shit happens' – and by this I mean when nurturing is neither enough nor appropriate – the predisposition for decisive action in effective leaders is seen. Once dealt with, the leaders I respect are seen to be straight back to their core task.

Leadership is a serving relationship that has the effect of facilitating human development.

Ted Wood

We need to move out of an era where you have a leader and lots of followers – into one where a leader is a leader of leaders.

John Adair

I believe that we learned that leadership is the most exquisite art that, practised at its optimum, transcends all other artistic media in its concurrent intricacies and simplicity. It is the art of making a big difference, be that with an individual or a society.

Leadership is a much-abused terminology in contemporary culture. In my construct, the one we addressed in *TACT*, it derives its vigour and strength from the bottom up – through the development of shared vision and mission. In the wider culture I am afraid that leadership is too frequently simply associated with securing compliance with the diktats of the powerful, whether in business or government. In the latter case it is all too often concerned with the delivery of policies that would be far more relevant and powerful had they been devised as locally as possible. I continue to observe this style of 'leadership' in my daily work. My word for what I see is 'administration', and barely that. For me leadership involves generating wide enthusiasm for a vision. It seems to me that securing control and delivering externally set targets dominates the agenda of contemporary boardrooms that are, incidentally, populated with detail people – skilled in accounting, systems and law. Maybe our boardrooms need more 'artists' and our institutions would benefit from nurturing non-conformists and contrarians – as I believe we used to.

As described earlier, we had found that the leaders and practitioners who contributed the most to enabling people to experience inclusion had entrepreneurial characteristics. Whilst undertaking this research we had inadvertently discover.

the most likely catalysts were senior operational leaders

operational managers of projects with wide objectives and

significant scope for innovation and true autonomy. We also

observed that the people who were getting included lifestyles

were also generally benefiting from services that scored highly

against the inspectors' measures despite the fact that these

were not particularly key measures for the leaders. They were

far more focused on the person and their happiness. From this

we observed yet another paradox.

Those concerned with control and compliance seem to believe

that effectiveness is enhanced by tight job specifications,

systematised policies and procedures, and lots of conformity.

This seemed to characterise the approach of regulators and

commissioners to standards and quality and was evident in their

paperwork. We observed that our top leaders simply served

people before systems. From time to time the compliance

people beat them up, usually over perceived bureaucratic

shortcomings. The organisational response was to agree that it

was necessary to 'render unto Caesar' but to ask specifically for

observations about the quality of life of the people served. The

intention was to educate but, in a minimum standards

environment, it was not a response, with hindsight, that was

likely to make friends. Our culture of continuous performance

improvement evolved towards social accounting and throughout grounded upon what people told us and what we knew from our relationships with them. The systems derived by regulators are in large part derived from what has gone wrong in history or is identified as a significant threat through generic risk assessments. When support staff are leading the implementation of arrangements that they have actively contributed to in respect of a person to whom they have made a personal commitment they are, in my experience, as likely to make a drug administration error or bath thermometer oversight as is a parent for their child or a daughter for her ageing mother. The standards are set for arrangements where there is no consistency of staffing, little personal commitment or loyalty to the people served, and little knowledge of them either. For me the minimum standard that *should* apply is that this state of affairs does not fulfil the standard and that the service should be deregistered.

In most hierarchies, even high employees do not leader anyone anywhere, in the sense of pointing out the direction and setting the pace. They simply follow precedents, obey regulations and move at the head of the crowd.

Lawrence J Peter – 'The Peter Principle'

A Learning Summary

Leading *TACT* from its inception through nearly 15 years of exponential growth and learning by doing, I derived conclusions about how we care for our vulnerable citizens (and many of us will ourselves one day be needy and vulnerable) that are at variance with the prevailing atmosphere of control, scarcity, distrust of citizens, and ill-founded dependence upon policies, systems and the expansionist professions.

And, when trawling the literature, I found that I was far from alone in drawing my contrarian conclusions. Experience and evidence abounds that demonstrates more positive and 'glass half-full' ways of doing things with better outcomes. Unfortunately it seems that the Social Services world and the political establishment is dominated by folk who are genetically predetermined to concentrate on trying not to get things wrong in what they perceive to be a malign environment rather than working towards a vision based upon trusting in the essential goodness and talents of their fellows.

I have asked lots of people to consider the following list and, to date, no-one has found any of the propositions contentious. Indeed, many have asserted that it amounts to 'common sense'.

And yet, despite assertions that everything is evidence-based, most of what seems to matter is in reality counter-cultural. My own take on this is that it is not only the professions but also the political class that have occupied 'territory' that is naturally the domain of the citizen and, through associations, civil society. Then, having assumed power, they cannot totally evade responsibility for the 'poisoned chalice' that they have naïvely invented. Readers will draw their own conclusions.

Suffice it to say that I learned that:

- Most challenging or, more accurately, distressed behaviour exhibited by people who have acquired very challenging reputations is instigated by the uninformed, thoughtless, naïve, or occasionally malicious actions of carers or organisations.
- Similarly, a large element of unacceptable behaviour and underperformance from staff members – at all levels in organisations – can be associated with a non-recognition of their gifts, denial of opportunities for self-expression and similarly uninformed and inappropriate behaviours by their employers.
- In the human services arena we should nurture leadership throughout our arrangements and organisations. People are not predictable and people who work with people need to be able to adapt and

problem solve. Moreover, they need to feel trusted to be responsive if they are to be both effective and accountable. Checklists and procedures are all well and good for standard processes and are useful in limited aspects of work with people. However, a systems perspective based upon a negative view of care workers is far too dominant and has perverse, if predictable, consequences.

o   Most of the folk we serve have important gifts and potentials that are indefensibly neglected. This is equally true of the people employed to provide care and support. This book is replete with stories of how things change when peoples' talents are liberated. Social care is morbidly preoccupied with deficits and deficiencies. We need to change our mindset and concentrate upon working with everyone's gifts.

o   Organisations that aspire to restore choice and control to the folk they serve will find this very difficult and probably impossible to achieve unless the same ethic is applied to the employees who are charged with sustaining an empowering environment.

o   Choice and control without loving and trustworthy people to help you exercise it and access to creative and positive thought is a kiss without the frisson.

o   No matter how hard we try, the natural form for the service is an institution – an organism with its own rules and mores, a workplace, an implicit or explicit hierarchy that cannot help but strive for dominance and permanence. The only defence against the primacy of the institution is outsiders who may not be tied by its conventions. People who are significantly dependent upon services need strong relationship networks. Representative advocacy is an anaemic and usually temporary alternative.

o   Loneliness, isolation and social exclusion are prevalent amongst those who are dependent upon social care services and are exacerbated by that dependency. If we address these issues, peoples' dependencies upon services is diminished and the associated costs likewise.

o   Small is functional.

o   The activity of caring for each other has little to learn from business – what it has learned has been largely pernicious.

We will be unable to create the core economy of the future so long as we live in a bifurcated world where all social problems are relegated either to paid professionals or to volunteers whose role is typically restricted to functioning as volunteers in the silos of the non-profit world.

It will take massive labour of all kinds to build the core economy of the future – an economy based on relationships and mutuality,

on trust and engagement, on speaking and listening and caring –
and above all on authentic respect. We will not get there by
expanding an entitlement system which apportions public
benefits based on negatives and deficiencies: what one lacks,
what disability one has, what misfortune one has suffered.

Professor Edgar Cahn in the foreword to Co-production - A
Manifesto for growing the core economy New Economics
Foundation 2008

Some Big Ideas -
LivesthroughFriends

Let's be clear. I don't believe that any of us — as service recipients — benefit, on balance, if the only people involved in our daily lives are paid to be there. Further, I am convinced that the commoditization or marketization of functions that would normally and appropriately be undertaken by caring friends and relatives and reciprocal interdependent communities are reflections of a dysfunctional and unsustainable economic system and an erosive consumerist cancer that is gnawing at the very humanity of our culture. It seems to me that it is crucial that we reinvent social interdependency, individual self-reliance, and a less materialistic and acquisitive mindset well before the inevitability of the system's collapse, when permanent sustained economic growth is experienced as a destructive and exploitative mythology. If we do not, there is a real risk that our society will decline into chaos – 'devil take the hindmost!'

So how do we do this? For sure I don't pretend to an answer but, as evidenced by the brief contributions that animate these pages, there are a lot of thinkers and doers grappling creatively with the issues.

A time for integrity

I guess that – in setting the scene in order that society (that is individuals and communities) can be major contributors to the necessary reinvention – it is essential that politicians and policy makers abandon short-termism and obfuscation, and acknowledge the simple fact that a combination of serious environmental, economic, political, and material challenges are progressively making our contemporary way of life unsustainable. It is time for a leadership with vision, that ditches the contentious notion that it is primarily the business of government to provide and manage services, and understands that great leaders inspire people to pull together, demonstrating a preference for animation over regulation, and nurturing and understanding the abundance of resources, material and of the spirit, that great leaders engage but can rarely ethically control.

A time for trust

Trusting people as the experts in their own lives and to make best use of the community's shared resources to which, in the case of social care funds, most have contributed royally, seems to me to be a non-negotiable. When self-direction and individual or personal budgets were canvassed in a succession of consultative and guidance documents it seemed clear that government's intention (and this seemed to have across the board support) was explicitly to take powers from the social care bureaucracies and put them back in the hands of individuals. It was a radical policy to roll back the invasion of the machinery of government in to the lives of citizens. What went with it was a clear steer that social care bureaucracies should and would become progressively more efficient, more focused, smaller and less costly. Repeated injunctions to develop preventative and carers' support initiatives with resources freed from administration reinforced the message.

Over the years the terminology applied to both keynote documents and pilot projects have illustrated the progressive dilution of the individual empowerment agenda. This has been in part due to the inevitability that it is generally not a plausible idea to expect organisations to significantly disempower and downsize themselves. This is a pretty disastrous example of incompetence on the part of a government that aspires to managerial excellence but it is dwarfed by the built-in self-destruct mechanism that is a continued application of a totally discredited fair access to care (FACS) process that perversely acts to ensure that people who need not become heavily dependent upon social care – with substantial and critical needs – almost certainly will.

The recent Green Paper took a small step in recognising that a great many of us will have need of social care support and should have the certainty of knowing that we have, via our taxes, stored up a secure entitlement to a government contribution totalling, on average, around a third of our predicted requirements. It seems to me that this may be a tentative step towards the approach that we should have started with in respect of a transparent scale of financial entitlements associated with self-direction.

There seems to be a persistent anomaly underlying the generation and implementation of social care policy. In businesses of all sorts there is a common approach to the structuring of organisations. We, the 'executive' (usually following extensive discussions with all our 'stakeholders'), decide what goals and targets we must achieve and then apply our resources as best we can to achieve our aspirations. There are usually dire consequences associated with a lack of disciplined implementation.

Government often fails to apply this discipline. As a starting point it usually breaks the first rule of project management or, in the context of *LivesthroughFriends'* methodology, 'making a difference through effective thinking'. All too often, and this has been persistently so in respect of the self-direction agenda, it is fluffy and imprecise, far from explicit, in respect of its goals. The immediate impact of this is that it encourages the most powerful stakeholders – those who administer the system – enormous scope to redefine policy in accordance with their own priorities.

I would assert that fundamental questions underlie the intention of transferring powers from social care bureaucracies to individuals. These include:

o   What, in stark terms, will the new arrangements look like?

o   In particular, what part will public funding play in meeting the social care and social security requirements of the population in the unfolding future?

o   Can anyone describe the quality of life that we should all expect if and when we become dependent on the support of others?

o   What sort of society does government aspire to encourage?

o   How will government actively promote the realisation of its societal aspirations?

- Do social care agencies have a role to play in disbursing funds to individuals?
- Or should social care payments be administered as a Benefit?
- How can we best employ the talents of social care professionals?
- How do we end the perverse rationing culture – that leaves people more dependent than they need to be?
- Having recognised that Local Government procurement does not usually operate in the interests of individuals, is there a continuing valid role for social care commissioning?
- What structures/organisations do we need to deliver our vision?

And these are just for starters!

Instead, government and its civil service machinery seem to have offered up a notion of self-direction and a radical re-invention of social care arrangements and expected those with the most to lose not to justify and rationalise their current practices and mindsets, and to find all manner of reasons to demonstrate their centrality to the success of a, by now, emasculated policy.

The lack of clarity in the government's stance leaves the most important stakeholders – the tax-paying public – ill-informed and ill-equipped to challenge the revisionist utterances of the special project teams that are set up to realise 'Transforming Social Care' or 'Putting People First'. Indeed, in our experience, the teams are far from welcoming of an independent interpretation and often reluctant to engage with those who espouse an individual, family, or community empowerment interpretation.

It is a shame that our 'leaders' have lacked the courage to enthusiastically describe and promote the vision that is sometimes explicit but more frequently implicit and compromised in their documents. I think that they know that the current system is unsustainable. I don't think they know that the population is pretty savvy, alive to the realities of life, and able to contribute to the creation of their own solutions to future challenges if only government would let them in on the facts and the action.

At *LivesthroughFriends* we have a 'toolkit', not for those who have historically administered and been the gate-keepers of the social care system, but for individuals and those who want to assist individuals who self-direct and choose to assume control and responsibility for their own lives or the lives of those they love.

The *LivesthroughFriends* 'toolkit' is simple and accessible.

A different mindset

We start from the perspective that self-direction offers the possibility to address the things that really matter to us rather than to have our needs re-interpreted into the products and services that businesses already provide.

In addition, as I have explained at length in earlier pages, I believe that in looking to the market for a model for how to provide 'social care', we effectively divorced ourselves from our humanity and were suckered into being wage slave consumers with little capacity left to be neighbours, carers and citizens. However, we have learned that institutions cannot care – they only provide services – and if we want care we need to look to each other.

John McKnight, who has been struggling with these issues for decades, puts it so clearly. Here is Martin Simon's summary of what he said when opening an event in Nova Scotia in the Summer of 2009:

There is a new worldwide movement developing, made up of people with a different vision for their local communities.

It is a hand-made, home-made vision. And wherever we look it is a culture that starts the same way.

First, we see what we have – individually, as neighbours and in this place of ours.

Second, we know that the power of what we have grows from creating new connections and relationships among and between what we have.

Third, we know that these connections happen when we individually or collectively act to make the connections – they don't just happen by themselves.

We also know that these three steps can often be blocked by great corporate, governmental, professional and academic institutions. They often say to us, "You are inadequate, incompetent, problematic or broken. We will fix you".

We ignore these voices and strive to be citizens – people with the vision and power to create a culture of community capacity, connection and care.

Locally we are the site of care. Institutions can only offer service – not care. We cannot purchase care. Care is the freely given commitment from the heart of one to another. As neighbours, *we care for each other. We care for children. We care for our elders. And it is this care that is the basic power of a community of citizens. Care cannot be provided, managed or purchased from systems.*

Fortunately, at the heart of our movement are three universal and abundant powers.

The giving of gifts – the gifts of the people in our neighbourhoods are boundless

The power of association – in association we join our gifts together and they become amplified, magnified, productive and celebrated.

Hospitality – we welcome strangers because we value their gifts and need to share our own.

There is no limit to our gifts, our associations and our hospitality.

Imagine that you are moving into a new family home. You are the first people to live in this property. The developers have left it to you to decide what to do with the garden. It is little more than a bare rectangle of topsoil that will soon be populated with weeds and briars if you leave things too long.

So, what will you do? You put some cash aside to deal with garden when you bought the house – for plants, hard landscaping, storage, and possibly to pay contractors – but this is not the total of your assets. You are a keen gardener as is your partner. You are moving with a comprehensive range of gardening tools and machinery. You are a member of the horticultural society and for years have exchanged plants, seeds and cuttings with other enthusiasts. While you have a preference for ornamental gardens, your brother is a self-sufficiency enthusiast and has an allotment. He has learned a lot from his friends at the allotments where lots of jobs, like winter cultivation and lifting main crop potatoes, are communal efforts. So, you aren't on your own and there are a lot of people who will help you with information, advice and practical assistance.

This is the first time you have had the challenge of a virgin piece of land; your first opportunity to pursue your own vision rather than adapt to the choices made by previous householders. You have watched gardening programmes on the television and taken an interest in garden design. Now you have not just the opportunity but also the necessity to attend to design. You know that if you don't you will regret it later. So you read the more accessible garden design books, trawl the internet for information, talk with your friends and acquaintances and, discovering a local evening class on the subject, your partner and yourself sign up.

Design, you soon discover, begins with an exploration of the functions that the garden will need to serve. Will it be a playground for children or an outdoor space for dogs? Do you want to grow fruit or vegetables, to keep poultry or bees, to make your own compost? Will you need facilities for propagation, protecting seedlings, or housing tender plants? Is your dream a decorative and architectural wonder that makes your visitors gasp with awe? Have you always had a yen for running water or a shaded pool with cruising carp? Is this to be an active place or a haven of retreat? Do you want to work on its maintenance everyday or as little as possible? Will the design need to accommodate changes over time, either by being amenable to adaptation or planned with a view to the time when bending and heavy lifting may be beyond your compass?

Design, when you are really clear about what really matters to you, is usually challenged by constraints. Is the site really amenable to your vision? Can all the resources you need be accessed? What are the top priorities? Can these competing priorities all be served? Successful design is not defeated by the constraints. It finds ways around obstructions or reconceives the project so that the obstruction no longer applies. Most of us have no confidence that we have the talents to resolve hard design problems. So our dreams and visions stay locked in our imaginations. In our garden analogy this means that, for most of us, we'll settle for an outcome that doesn't require too much problem solving or innovation. If we are very affluent we might buy the services of a top designer but even they will not grasp and realise our vision, not that they could not, but because they are driven by their own imaginations. The hindering thinking that tells us that we are not up to the challenges is reinforced by the increasingly powerful message that 'creatives' are specially talented people, that in areas beyond the mundane in our lives we need to patronise 'experts' and 'professionals', and that our options have to be defined by what they can do. There are many areas of life, like medicine and the law, where we cannot avoid the need to 'intelligently' trust specialists but this, in my view, cannot and should not be universally applied to how we envision our lives with a disability, chronic sickness, or frailty.

We are clear that just about everyone has the capacity to be imaginative and to realise their vision in a far more satisfying way. The 'toolkit' sets out a step by step approach to effective and creative thinking, problem solving, and making the most of serendipity that is for everyone and involves no 'rocket science'. We are heavily indebted to our friends, Andy Gilbert and Ian Chakravorty, at *Go MAD Thinking*. Their beautifully accessible approach is fundamental to *LivesthroughFriends*' support to self-direction.

Mindset is, in our experience, at the core of planning and organising our own care and support or assisting others to do so:

- Recognising self-direction as a continuing opportunity to develop bespoke and progressive ways of supporting the best life we can imagine.
- A fierce commitment to individual autonomy and well-informed self-determination.
- Seeing ourselves or our clients in a social context – not as a customer in need of services – 'The Social Model'.
- And, in this knowledge, intentionally networking in our/their community.
- Knowing that money is only part of the resource package and seeking out the care that services do not provide.
- Being open to involving others – people are always the solution in one way or another.
- Working from an assumption of interdependency and seeking out opportunities to contribute as well as receive.
- Understanding that 'if we always do what we've always done, we'll always get what we always got'. Choosing to be intentionally and skilfully creative. Choosing to attend to our thinking.
- Being always aware that we have all been socialised in a market-driven society and thinking through our relationship with services when we choose to engage with them.

o   *Realising, if you spend your life assisting others to achieve their 'good life', that it is part and parcel of the job to be positive, optimistic, resourceful and hospitable. We are animateurs, we breathe life into dreams. We don't just turn on a bulb, we should be the light.*

But before we consider the realisation of our hopes and dreams we need to be clear about, "What", with acknowledgement to the Spice Girls, "I really, really want".

Asking a Different Question

LivesthroughFriends is classically entrepreneurial. Our key characteristic - within a vision of interdependent communities, the abolition of neglectful loneliness and isolation, and people who are more self-reliant and less state dependent – is a capacity to recognise and connect with other peoples' great insights, ideas and practices and apply them in our context.

Earlier I introduced *PLAN*, Vickie Cammack and Al Etmanski and, in particular, the power of their simple question:

Instead of asking, "What programmes and services do you need? - you might instead ask, "What is a good life for you?"

We have been asking a wide spectrum of people, including lots of variously disabled or frail elderly folk, that question over the past 3 or 4 years and no matter who is asked or where (I have asked the question in most EU and applicant countries as well as in the UK) there is a stunning similarity of responses and peoples' priorities are very consistent.

o   **Relationships** – 'loving, caring, intimate, unconditional, friendships, family, children, parents, etc.' – invariably figure as first amongst priorities and the bedrock issue.

When we unpick the feelings and thoughts behind the words we cannot but appreciate the intensity with which we, the human race, need to belong, to be interdependent, to be loved, to be valued, to have a giving role. This is central to our wellbeing, to our survival. When we belong we look out for each other. When we are alone and isolated, a beneficiary rather than a loved one, even in a quite benign environment, we feel vulnerable. Think about it... why do we visit people in hospital?

o   **Financial Security – to be 'comfortable'**

We feel unsafe and insecure if we don't have folk looking out for us. We feel at least as vulnerable if we can't put a roof over our heads and food on the table and, respondents tell us, very insecure if we do not have the means within our control to escape dependency upon the decisions of others. Being 'comfortable' seems to be about having the means to make our own choices and to have the ability to change our circumstances if we wish without reference to any 'authority'.

To some extent the Personalisation agenda is a welcome recognition of everyone's essential need for a degree of socio-economic autonomy. However, the implementation of personal budgets and self-direction, assuming that the principles survive reinterpretation during implementation, has to coexist with financial assessment policies and charging rules that essentially either make or leave those entitled to social care funding poor. While the 2009 Green Paper and subsequent PM statements about the 'National Care Service' seem to acknowledge resource challenges and propose new arrangements, they remain naïvely and unjustifiably wedded to the service culture, neglectful of the community and our people, and insensitive to the fact that people can make a better job of caring than government.

It is a simple fact of life that a consequence of our historic approach to social security and the welfare state has been a strong correlation between disability, dependency and poverty. There's been a fierce determination to ensure that the State should not pay for anything that an individual has the means to provide for himself and hence, paradoxically, a built-in disincentive to self-reliance. This perverse consequence of the benefits system has permeated the social care system as systems have replaced social and community work. Sometimes I cannot discern a difference between the prevalent cultures in the benefits and social care arenas. When resources are stretched – as we always feel they are – we (the professionals) are drawn to deal with 'life and limb' rather than a 'good life' and, in doing what we have always done, can become cynical and emotional and intellectually wizened. 'Working the system' for our client supersedes 'changing the system', and too soon we become apologists for the immutable, cogs in the wheel.

Personalised budgets have the potential to put a little wealth and therefore an element of choice and autonomy in the hands of disabled people. Used creatively they have the potential to be used to assist people to break out of or significantly diminish their welfare dependency. However, just as was evidenced when Direct Payments regulations were introduced, it does not take long for the bureaucracy to warn of fraud and abuse and iteratively introduce reactive rules for the protection of 'public funds'. I have a strong suspicion that for every fraudster or abuser there are ten, twenty or fifty good folk who, given the chance - given trust, respect, and empowering help – might begin to make a real difference. I would always rank the interests of the good citizens above the prosecution of the odd offender. However, we seem to live a time that lacks perspective.

In December 2009 in Canada, a federal Disability Savings Fund was enacted whereby the State not only encourages disabled people to have personal wealth and choice but actively contributes to the build-up of savings on a matched dollars basis that is scaled to benefit the poorest families to the greatest degree. The legislation was introduced for really practical reasons:

- Families who were finding ways around the previous legislation in order to help their relative have the benefit of assets;

- Seemed to be assisting their relative to enjoy a much more included, contributing, and happy life;

- While, over time, the same people seemed to be less significantly dependent upon publicly funded services.

With help from *PLAN* and associated campaigners the federal government understood that everyone would benefit from government stepping back and helping rather than seeking to plan, command and control. This feels like a remarkably mature political environment to me. I wonder how long it will take for the penny to drop that, instead of closing loopholes and hoovering up every bit of tax and income it can, marked societal and humanitarian benefits would be derived from the UK Treasury supporting disabled people in the UK to accumulate wealth, exercise choice, and be active in our economy?

o   **A Contributing Citizen**

After permanently disabling strokes Merlin's passionate goals were to find ways to be a good husband and responsible parent and to have a new career, 'helping people'. We helped him to found a time bank initiative.

In planning to move on from a specialist autism service Geoff encapsulated his vision for his future as, "I want to pay tax!" When I recovered from a fit of giggling he told me that it was a matter of self esteem. "When you are dependent for everything you get treated like a non-person, second class citizen. If you feel like a second class person you just let it happen – then I obsess about it and get ill." I understood. As I got to know Geoff better I was the beneficiary of his hospitality, kindness and insights. He understood far better than I that real citizenship is contingent. As citizens we justify our rights by meeting our responsibilities. As human beings our survival depends upon reciprocity.

Bill was 89, frail, vulnerable and feeling that this 'dying business takes an awful long time'. One of his daughters was struggling to support Bill and her husband's demented mother and Bill feels 'a burden'. He was lonely and isolated. His house and garden were run down and neglected. Bill was depressed.

Bill has a history. As well as being a family man he has been a skilled engineer (steam in ships and railway locomotives, and model making), an ace match angler, and a prize-winning gardener and allotment holder. He had been the primary carer for his wife during her long, last illness and concurrently lost contact with old work and hobby colleagues and aged. He won't have anything to do with 'charity'. He sabotaged the domiciliary services arranged by his daughter by insisting that what he needed was company not cleaning.

Bill's priorities were about seeing people. His daughter's were about his safety, cleanliness, regular meals and renovating the house. We helped him to share his gifts – by facilitating his 'reconnection' with his work/steam railways, angling and horticultural life. We also helped his daughter to bring Bill's very large, 4-generation, extended family together to celebrate his 90th birthday. Getting people back into Bill's life had lots of spin-offs. His garden, a small patch at the front of his townhouse and a great source of shame for Bill, was a picture, sorted by friends and equipped with a bench so that Bill could sit out on nice days and chat with neighbours. Friends redecorated his hall and stairwell. He got to go fishing again... and had the company he desired.

When we think of social care and needs assessments how often do we recognise that an absolutely fundamental need of human beings is to be needed, to be respected, to reciprocate? And how often does it cross our minds that by addressing this need we will very often ensure that other needs are incidentally met?

Experience tells me that it is invariably the case that if we have friends and valued roles in our lives we are pretty rich... in social capital. Naysayers will invariably, at this point, describe somebody who could not possibly have friends nor own any gifts. I respond with the fact that I have yet to meet anyone like their acquaintance but that, if there is a small population of such impoverished and uncared for folk, their existence should not dissuade us from addressing the real aspirations of the massive majority. What, of course, the objectors are often really saying is that they don't see gifts and value in disabled people, which is worrying because they are often service staff or relatives.

I first met Tony nearly 40 years ago. In his early 30s he had been admitted to the psycho-geriatric admission ward of a mental hospital – and there he stayed. Under treatment for depression he had been prescribed some medication and been given clear instructions about not drinking alcohol or taking certain foods. He had and the adverse reaction had literally blown his mind, resulting in irreversible brain damage and blindness. His marriage was on the rocks before these events and both his parents were dead. He seemed to have no-one. Worse, Tony was seen as vicious and dangerous. He spent most of his day standing, feet apart, head thrown back, rocking. If people engaged with him he would cling to them and not let go and grip on harder if they tried to disengage. This would often escalate, particularly if the person he was clinging to was a very confused old gentleman who had started to panic and become aggressive – a frequent occurrence. The more frenetic the situation, the harder Tony would hang on and, if attacked, his reaction was to bite. The 'clinical' response was chemical and made not a lot of difference and, of course, no-one in those days seemed to be thinking about how Tony would spend the rest of his life. In the three years I was training in that group of hospitals he lived on the psycho-geriatric admission ward.

But a mature nursing assistant was thinking and she put the clinicians to shame. The care team could be distinguished within the hospital by their bruised hands and arms. If anything, things were getting worse and Tony seemed to be increasingly marginalised and neglected. She began to analyse Tony's behaviour. In particular she imagined what it would be like to be Tony. She visualised a frightening life of darkness and confusion, of surprises, of loneliness, of frustrated sexuality, of intimacy denied, and of powerlessness. She interpreted Tony's need to grip hold as a request, a plea for reassurance, as a response to panic.

I don't think she attended evening classes or read psychology tomes. Instead, when engaging with Tony she made a point of introducing herself, talking quietly about what was going to happen and, having taken his hand, organising things so that they could sit together stroking and massaging his gripping hand

and forearm while she explained again about dinner, shaving, going to the toilet or whatever else was on the immediate agenda. Fragrant hand cream became part of the ritual and it was quickly evident that she was developing a trusting relationship with Tony, and in no time other women in the team were following her lead. (These were macho times and I blushingly recall the clumsily self-conscious efforts of us lads but it didn't take long for some of us to find our sensitive sides!)

So far so good. The ward had what seemed to be a semi-resident population of old men's wives, many of whom visited almost daily, and who constituted a mutual support society for themselves and often us as well. They had been very concerned about and frightened of Tony – fearing both for themselves and their husbands. Visits to people who no longer recognise or know you had become bearable for many because of group support and the ladies were very much part of the care team and contributed a lot to creating a family atmosphere for 2 or 3 hours most afternoons. Almost subliminally it seemed that they absorbed the new care regimen for Tony and, just as they would for everyone else, if a staff member needed to leave Tony mid-activity to sort out someone else's needs, a voice would chirp up assuring us that Tony would be seen to while we were away. Out of the blue Tony acquired a 'harem' of replacement 'mums' who ensured that he had a birthday and Christmas, walks in the grounds on sunny days, and who, over time, replaced his hospital clothing with his own wardrobe. Tony, for sure, added meaning to their lives and rewarded them with his attention and simple being. Everyone has gifts!

o **A Place of My Own**

In my experience, lots of people get stuck at 'Maslow base camp' in their thinking about the idea of home. In the twinkling of an eye the issue is reframed as housing and in no time the concrete thinking of affordability, units, housing benefit rates and sharing dominate. There is nonetheless a national shortage of housing to rent and a sea of counter-productive regulation and red tape that acts as a disincentive to housing providers in all sectors to provide adapted accommodation. Government, national and European, would, in my view, serve us far better if it attacked these structural problems rather than dreaming up more perverse regulations.

We need to start out on this journey from a different place. Instead of asking, "what sort of housing will you need", on those occasions where the acquisition of somewhere else to live is part of the brief, we start with the question, "How do you want to live".

This is a much easier question to ask of someone who has lived a relatively full autonomous life previously, although many of us are conditioned to associate acquired dependency with being a burden and, hence, will look to what they perceive to be in the best interests of those carrying the burden. In doing so they often fail to appreciate that their 'sacrifice' may only heighten the feelings of guilt and loss experienced by their loved ones.

It is far more difficult to ask and explore with someone whose limited life experience is derived from restrictive, over-protective, or segregated 'care'.

That being said, it is worth spending time getting as clear an idea as you can because where someone lives is pretty fundamental to their support plan and you should not compromise the foundations. If someone lives in a setting where the culture is contrary to the thrust of the plan you will spend lots of time fighting losing battles.

"How do you want to live?" gets to grips with what really matters. A wide range of issues come up and individuals demonstrate very different priorities. It is a mistake to assume we all want to live the same way. Surely we know this already? Vickie Cammack tells the story of a woman who, after a long experience of services, moved into her own home. She jubilantly explained that, for the first time in her life she was able to, "take off her mask and hang it on the peg with her coat", when she got home. "I feel as though I can be myself – no-one keeps records about me or works at my house like it's a care home. I employ my PA's, they support me and I set the rules".

Jon wants life to be one continuous party. He loves it when folk call in for tea and a chat. He begged a job delivering the local free newspaper as an excuse to doorstep his neighbours and get to know them. His current project, aided by an entrepreneurial support worker recruited through a friendship made at the local allotments, is to provide a seasonal vegetable box service to his neighbours from his plot. Jon holds a coffee morning every month to raise funds for the local youth café – a clever idea thought up by a neighbour after Jon confided that he felt intimidated by groups of young people and avoided going out at night because of 'the gangs'. Now Jon is a welcome visitor at the café and is sharing his gardening interest with a group of youngsters who are engaging with a transition towns project. Jon hopes to acquire more growing land and more friends and collaborators through this. The planning meetings are happening around his kitchen table, as are the meetings of the recently reinvigorated community watch.

When Jon was asked, "How do you want to live?" it was quickly apparent that his good life involved sociability and hospitality. The specification for Jon's place included statements such as:
o   at the heart of a neighbourhood;
o   outgoing and sociable support people;

o   space to entertain – a kitchen table;

o   with people of a similar nature, otherwise his own place;

o   a garden or access to an allotment nearby.

Lots of options were explored but Jon was in no doubt when we found a ground floor flat in a converted town house in a long established central area of terraced streets at a rent that would be covered by housing benefit. The selling point was the spacious Victorian kitchen. The local shops, fortuitously free plots at the allotments just 400 yards away, and the fact that the lady delivering the post engaged us in conversation (as she did with others wherever, surprisingly often, doors were opened as she progressed along the street) closed the deal.

Such an arrangement would not have suited Doreen, a fiercely independent and opinionated 86-year-old spinster who had come nearly to death's door as a result of a stubborn refusal to ask for help from the many people who cared about her but were kept firmly at arm's length. Following a long period of hospitalisation the time came for planning next steps. Doreen insisted she was dying and the medics replied that they were not aware of any terminal illness, just frailty and the fruits of time. Doreen had also convinced herself that she was fast dementing, this having roots in both the confusion resulting from her recent toxic state and her pre-occupation with the mental health problems that had been the lot of her parents.

Doreen had lived on her own for nearly fifty years in a small country town in a convenient bungalow, new when she bought it. Apart from a couple of neighbours, her closest friends lived in communities across four counties and her few near relatives often further afield. Doreen had adopted a very self-reliant and self-engrossed way of life. Her friends and relatives were important to her and she enjoyed their company, was an engaging hostess and attentive friend, but she never stayed over or holidayed with friends. Enough would be enough and she would go home or have set the timescale subtly for her visitors to leave when they visited her. In later life she employed a gardener, engaged cleaning companies for occasional deep cleans but never regular visits, and even booked herself for respite weeks at a local residential home 'for a rest'.

It took several attempts to persuade Doreen to engage with the question of what next in her life. She would be too tired, telling me that I must decide, or too confused or 'nutty' (as she would put it), giving me Christmas cards inscribed with bizarre and sometimes hurtful messages to send to people as she would be dead, or expressing apparently paranoid ideas about visitors and hospital staff. In due course the pressure was on. Christmas was imminent. There was no reason for Doreen to be in hospital. I visited. Doreen had just been moved from a side room into what I perceived to be the confusing hurly burly of the Nightingale ward. She was agitated and appeared distressed and confused. I tried, gently, to engage her over the future without success. I sought help from the nursing staff; was there a quiet place where I could talk with Doreen? They were stretched. I was a nuisance. Nothing transpired. Eventually I wrote a brief note saying that:

- I had checked out domiciliary care agencies who would be able to deliver personal assistance at home – and here were details of a couple that I believed would prove reliable.

- I had explored the possibility and cost associated with employing a live-in carer/companion and thought that this was a viable option but that this would take some time to organise.

- If the live-in option appealed, interim arrangements could be made via a domiciliary care arrangement or a short-term contract with a residential or nursing home – however, I could not vouch for the quality of the homes prepared to take on short-term arrangements.

- I had checked out immediate vacancies in a number of private nursing homes whose good reputations were confirmed by my personal knowledge and experience. Two had a vacancy and competing demands. One was near to two of Doreen's relatives, the other easily accessible to everyone who would travel to see her. In both cases (it was a Friday) the Homes would hold the room until Monday.

- I also confirmed that, with her permission, I had spoken with her solicitor who had confirmed that, "As long as Doreen doesn't live to be 130, money won't be a problem".

I left my note and some brochures on Doreen's bedside locker – by now Doreen appeared to be sleeping - and had a word with the Ward Manager on my way out to let her know where I had got to and asking that Doreen might be helped to think about the options. I said I would call in over the weekend and did, on my way home from a rugby match, on the Saturday evening.

When I arrived Doreen was awake and alert. Saying nothing she gave me a tatty piece of paper that she had been going to give to a nurse. On it she had boldly written, 'please ring Bob Rhodes and tell him that I want to go to...', and she had named one of the nursing homes. I told her that I was surprised, that everything I thought I knew about her indicated that she would want to go back to her own home, her own things, her routine.

She said, "I've been a stupid old woman. I have lain here willing myself to die and doing everything I could to avoid making a decision. I have pretended to be asleep, daft, anything to stop you asking me. I'm grateful that you didn't just decide for me.

You would have got it wrong. I cannot bear the thought of going home and having someone else in the house all the time. It would have to be paid people. My neighbours would want to help but they are both old and ill like me, and one has a husband with terminal cancer to care for. So the lesser of the evils is my own space, a private room, in a decent nursing home where, if I'm lucky and I don't offend them all, people will visit me."

The doctors were right and Doreen was not dying. For 6 months she persisted that it was taking her a long time to shake off her mortal coil, that she had not the energy to socialise, the concentration to read, and so on, but as summer blossomed so did Doreen's life. By then she had made some acquaintances – on her terms as usual - joined them for meals when it suited her and participated in occasional trips out. She was reading again – mainly the classics – and taking an interest in the comings and goings of the families in her life. I had been concerned that she would just lie back and wither – become institutionalised but the essential Doreen was back; self-reliant, independent, funny and self-deprecating, occasionally barbed and a little too honest, and quietly in charge. She is convinced she made the right choice.

A fundamental rule in life, and especially when you are planning your own social care or supporting someone else to do so, is to always leave yourself a get-out clause, an opportunity to change your mind when you find out that you've got something wrong.

When older people give up their homes, whether owned or rented, and move into communal care settings they are often 'burning their boats'. Once they have moved out and sold up, the system as a whole - beliefs, practices and rules – gives force to ageist assumptions that they have *à la Brave New World* (but a little older) moved into 'God's Waiting Room' and pathetically divested some of their humanity and most of their citizenship. Having already sanitized death and removed it and the process of dying from western societies' everyday experience we have, over the last three or four decades, effectively erased everyday experience of frail elderly people from most peoples' lives as well. Given that more and more of us are living into advanced old age this is not only unworthy of us but also incredibly short-sighted.

Ancient societies seem to have recognised the wisdom that accompanies great experience. In my youth, in a community where old age was naturally accommodated just as the needs and dependences of infancy and childhood were met, the very old were a constant source of gifts. They endowed a sense of heritage and belonging – passing on and adding to the oral history of the community. I learned gentleness, reflection, and the ability to take comfort from and work with uncertainty from older people and especially my grandfather. I absorbed a sense of interdependence, of responsibility for others, of duty, and of respect for people in general in a culture where it was normal to muck in, give and take, be hospitable, be 'askable' and ask. For the Support Broker who works to a 'good life' framework it is crucial that we ensure that the 'my place' choices that older people make do not obstruct their opportunities to maintain important relationships, share their gifts, be contributing citizens and be visible and therefore safer.

For government and policy makers – if you accept the challenge of facilitating an interdependent and kinder society – I would assert that action has to be taken to reverse the ghettoisation of older people and disabled younger people. When I was small, old people were scattered in my neighbourhood and I knew them. By the time I was a teenager a cul-de-sac of old peoples' bungalows had been built in what had previously been a farmyard near the centre of the village. This was immediately a no-go area as we had no-one to visit there and were told not to play on the green in front of the properties – the council had put a up 'no ball games' signs to ensure 'peace' for the old folk. It was as silent as the grave. We had begun to silo the very old in our community. As we respond, as eventually we must, to the growing housing shortage and, in particular, homes for folks with additional needs we need to ensure that we recreate mixed communities where old folk have young families for neighbours and disabled people have the benefit of neighbours who take an interest when the power is cut or a bulb needs changing.

o   **Safe and Sound – Who's looking out for You?**

Nobody enjoys feeling unsafe and too insecure for very long. It has physiological and psychological effects that in short bursts can be exhilarating but as a chronic condition are severely debilitating. So it is no surprise that when we ask people about their 'good lives' the issue of safety and security is generally explicit and always implicit.

When we ask folk what they need to feel safe they respond with a predictable list. They talk about:

- Love, intimacy, friends, family, belonging – feeling as though folks 'look out' for them.
- Being financially comfortable – having enough cash to make important choices.
- Being respected and accorded the rights and responsibilities of citizenship as a contributing member of the community.
- Having their own home or place in a proprietary way – **my** place.
- Enjoying good health – free of pain and nagging anxiety.

If I have all or most of these, they say, that makes me feel safe and secure. Strangely, no-one has yet responded by listing an effective police force, wonderful safeguarding arrangements, inspired social care regulators, the CRB nor the ISA, nor any form of direct government action.

Equally oddly, being loveless and lonely, unable to contribute to society, over-dependent and under-valued, and housed at the discretion of a service provider and hence feeling very insecure don't generate much of a score when a fair access to care eligibility 'assessment' is undertaken.

And I find it bizarre that we operate a social welfare and security system that says that there's no point in striving to be a contributing member of society because, no matter what you or others connected with you have contributed in taxation throughout your life, you will pay for the support you need until you are impoverished. Eventually we subscribe to a society that says that people who need social care must eventually be poor, dependent and insecure – and possibly unsafe as well.

This because, despite all the verbiage and posturing, the medical model dominates our concept of social care. The social model is so much hot air because it involves too much that cannot be priced and certainly not bureaucratically controlled and accounted for.

A Solid Reference Point and a 'Mindset' – a basis for Support Planning and Implementation

I referred to Maslow's *Index of Psychological Needs* earlier and, as I progressed my explanation of the 'good life' framework for self-direction, grew in awareness of the error one makes if one is insensitive to the interconnections and interdependencies between the superficially separate levels. Nearly all of the criteria set out in the pyramid can only be met in the context of our intimate and social relationships.

I use the 'good life' framework as one of the key reference points for my thinking and practice in the certainty that the first amongst equals is the necessity of loving relationships and a solid sense of belonging. In doing so I face the complications and downsides associated with interpersonal interactions square on. Too frequently I work with people with intellectual disabilities who are held back and deskilled by the low expectations, over-protectiveness and ignorance of their parents and siblings. Just as often we encounter families of older people where sibling rivalries, issues of inheritance, and the exploitation of the main carer completely dominate the starting agenda.

Those who believe that 'support brokerage', whatever that is, is a simple or technical matter of taking folks shopping in the social care marketplace are naïve and plainly wrong; not just because in doing this they are unlikely to address the most important issues for the 'focus person' and disregard key unpriced resources but, more importantly, when we support people to self–direct we invariably deal with competing needs and wills, and frequently need to work with conflict. This, I hasten to add, does not constitute a justification for professional 'experts' in conflict resolution. Families and communities had a remarkable capacity for resolving interpersonal conflicts before we professionalised things and made it someone else's responsibility. Interdependency encourages integrity and an acceptance of difference. It gives rise to tolerance, including a tolerance of plain speaking when this is seen to be done with helpful intent. Over and over again I see resolutions forged in real life by the peripheral actors who have no axe to grind and can see the wood for the trees. The broker or facilitator's task is often just to ensure that sensible relatives and friends are engaged in the process. As I have found too often to my and my client's cost, if the broker is the only interpreter and advocate of the 'focus person's' wishes unwanted compromises or stalemate result.

Underlying the 'good life' approach is a definite 'mindset'; an approach to life that, while it is founded in values and beliefs and highly principled, is unpretentious, inclusive and accessible – in John McKnight's memorable description, 'home-made and handmade'.

The 'mindset' is founded upon:

o   A feeling that people deserve bespoke responses to their individual circumstances, that off-the-peg solutions are manifestations of a society that knows the price of everything and the value of nothing.

o   Enthusiasm for personalised arrangements.

o   Being comfortable with evolution, learning by doing, trial and error, the flexibility of everyday life.

o   An appreciation of social history.

o   Reservations about the perverse consequences of the exponential and ill-considered application of the good intentions of the welfare state.

o   Doubts about the doctrine of 'fairness' – if that implies a transfer of power or loss of autonomy to arbitrary bureaucracy.

o   A fundamental belief in the present and potential resourcefulness, talents and kindness of individuals and communities.

o   A strong perception that the very essence of community is being stifled as an unacknowledged consequence of consumer society – 'the age of entertainment' as someone so succinctly described us.

- A healthy and ever more angry distrust of authority and institutions and a belief that the power of supposedly democratic institutions, bureaucrats and professionals has grown beyond reason.

- A belief that government should be more about nurture rather than control.

- The notion that government should disengage from trying to define and social engineer 'communities' and instead provide the scope and some unfettered means for people to generate their own models.

- A commitment to self-direction and self-determination – the restoration of power over their personal circumstances to individuals.

- A predisposition to work with peoples' gifts and competences.

- A willingness to support self-direction in a diversity of ways that build capacity with individuals and communities – recognising that the casework approach is one of many valid interventions.

- Concerns about the impact upon self-direction and the re-invention of interdependent communities if support brokerage is professionalised, marketized and 'silo'd' as another social care commodity.

- ○ Seeing the potential for revolutionary change implicit in the successive social care transformation agendas.
- ○ Understanding that this will be achieved by action, by demonstration, through stories and the emergence of a movement.

As things stand, advocates of the 'good life' are by definition out of step with the prevailing, contradictory, social care hegemony. As we, at *LivesthroughFriends*, encourage participants in our courses and events to look at the world through 'good life' eyes and to compare it to the medical model, deficit listing, and definitely not 'needs-led' fair access to care system, we invariably find the social, economic, and political perspectives set out in the above list fed back to us as, it might be described, common knowledge. I used to be reticent to share this analysis in 'polite company' for fear of being marginalized as some sort of extremist or fanatic. In due course I began to understand that people all know this stuff and only think that folk like me are a bit strange because we fantasise about changing things. The large majority of professionals I meet share most aspects of the analysis. They hate the systematisation, bureaucratisation and deskilling of their roles. They resent their disempowerment and the erosion of their professional responsibility to be accountable first and foremost to their clients, and the redefinition of their work as 'assessment monkeys'. They are, however, threatened by the notion that those in power will never take responsibility for their system and will blame and victimise the operatives. It happens every week, so their fears are justified. They are also legitimately concerned about job security, either if the market approach implodes or some aspects of our vision are implemented in a bastardised way. Professionals do not trust social care leaders who talk in acronyms, are uncritical of contradictory government targets, fail to lead, and offer no cogent vision.

You don't need a social research team or a TV documentary crew to find out how community has withered. Just fill a room with 50+s and listen, dropping in the odd high quality question to stimulate memories.

Essentially, people who facilitate full-blown self-direction aspire to help others define and achieve the life they want despite the rules, despite the inertia of the system, despite consumer culture. And they do not depend upon a procedure manual or detailed checklist – instead they rely on their resourcefulness, tenacity, creativity, networking and problem-solving skills, and cleave to an incremental and iterative or evolving working style. They don't have all the answers and don't expect to get all the ducks in a row immediately. They are committed to developing confidence and capacity in others. In *LivesthroughFriend's* work we make it clear that we do not deskill or obstruct the development of people by assuming roles that folk can undertake for themselves. We have all learned through trial and error, this is how we develop discernment, and take the view that people who have been denied those experiences earlier in life must be accorded the chance to learn from experience. Our task in all things is to seek to ensure, through advice, that no boats are burned and that mistakes can be remedied relatively painlessly. This seems a pretty sensible way to address life in general – home-made and handmade.

What's your Good Life about?
High Quality Questions

The practice of helping someone who needs support about the life to which they aspire is simply a matter of asking the right, high-quality questions. The prevailing splurge of self/joint/FAC/SP/ILF and related 'assessment questionnaires' are not framed to assist someone to get a life. Rather they are transparently designed to establish whether the respondent has disabilities or incapacities, largely of physical function, for which there is a costed service option and which fits into, as I have previously asserted, a largely medical model interpretation of what constitutes substantial or critical need. Despite the discussion around 'prevention and early intervention' and the regular feting of the 'big names' of asset-based community development at shop window events, the machinery of social care administration doesn't appear to have got the message that people with strong social and relationship networks make less demands on our mutual publicly-funded resources and are generally far happier than those who are forced to by dint of their isolation.

The broker or facilitator's role is to ask questions that get to the fundament of what makes life worth living for the focus person and, as a consequence of the process, uncovers possible ways of realising the person's aspirations. Here, through the medium of self-direction, we have the revolutionary opportunity to redefine social care from the client's perspective.

High quality questions are a product of active and very attentive listening. Many of us, me especially, are so passionate about our own agenda and get such a charge from innovating around it that when we should be sitting back and listening, probing and researching, we are instead generating lists of possibilities and proposals. I have had to learn that there will be plenty of opportunities to be the clever dick and suggest innovative connections and exciting solutions later on and that they will be all the more relevant because I took the time to listen, reflect and probe. And our questioning needs to lead to a comprehensive understanding of the person, their situation and their assets as well as their needs.

Just because we assert that the universal needs of humanity, as expressed in the 'good life' findings, must be addressed this does not mean that we don't need to know about and understand the person's daily living, physical, emotional and health needs. It is just that it is helpful to understand them as issues to be resolved in order that the individual can be helped to address their fundamental needs and as issues that are often of less moment if a basic need is satisfied.

The practice is not 'rocket science'. But it is about doing something unusual! Actually it is two unusual things. The first is very rare in these days of push button immediacy and episode targets – we give people as much uninterrupted and attentive time as is necessary. The second is that we do not ask people to justify their opinions and feelings – we don't ask "Why?" Instead we are interested in exploring around:

○ **What**... matters, worries, ideas, assets, organisations, might happen, etc...? **What should we sort out first?**

○ **Who**... could, does, arranges, makes, looks after, knows, visits, was, etc...? **Who would you like to help you plan this?**

○ **How**... might, does, could, much, about, often, many, did you, do, etc...? **How do you cope with housework and cooking now?**

○ **Where**... does, are, is, could you, etc...? **Where could I find out how to contact them?**

○ **When**... **shall we hold the party? What will we tell people in advance? Who shall we invite? How will we get their buy-in? Where will we hold it? What about an agenda? Who could we ask to do the catering? What clubs, groups and organisations are you/were you a member of? How might we get in touch with folk who**

know/would remember you? Where might we find an entertainer who would do it for free?

and following the strands of enquiry, 'digging down' (as I sought to briefly demonstrate above) and encouraging the person or their representatives to talk freely. If it is possible to involve others who are enabling, that is not seeking to take over the answering and the telling of the stories, this can be very helpful. And sometimes a bit of self-revelation - "I have to ask my wife how to set the central heating clock; it's too technical for me!" – gives licence for a bit more candour.

The greatest gift in assessment and information collection is the ability to mesh an unfolding succession of high quality questions within a relaxed conversation. Most of us resent and get spiky in the face of an inquisition. My friend Merlin, a proud and gentle man with severe disabilities resulting from a stroke, protested in tears that he felt 'violated – raped' when he completed a draft self-assessment questionnaire during a peer brokerage co-production series of events. "They are only interested in my inabilities, what I can't do. I'm still quite a young man. I want help to live, to help others, to contribute to my family". Earlier Merlin had thrown himself enthusiastically into a possibilities exercise that had explored his life and aspirations in the context of:

o   people and relationships;

o   financial security;

o   citizenship, contribution, self-reliance, self-respect...

o   and what would be necessary for him to feel safe and secure.

There were no pressing issues in relation to his home. Merlin has a loving and resourceful family, a strong partner, optimistic kids and his own home that, given his building background, is adapted. The crucial issue for Merlin is his insecurity and paranoia that wells up because he sees himself as a non-contributing burden. To find ways of contributing, to deserve the love and care of his family, this is the issue that Merlin wants the social care system to address. The 'good life' approach to high quality questioning enabled him to closely define the need as a problem that could be solved for the first time. No wonder that he was deflated and demoralised by the council's draft assessment.

That co-production group was very clear in their advice to their council. "Redesign your self-assessment process please. Let us tell you about the sort of life we want to live." The man from the council wasn't defensive, was clearly moved by what he heard, but was frank and honest about the practicalities of designing an assessment process that delivered both an eligibility test and a funding allocation based upon effective intervention.

I suggested that maybe the time was ripe to ask a high quality question or two?

Q: What are the possible key elements of your vision for a sustainable social care service?

Q: How might our vision require any changes to our 'culture' – are notions of interdependence and self-reliance a significant part of our vision?

Q: What might we possibly learn from Local Area Co-ordination and the Asset Based Community Development world in relation to our **mainstream** strategy?

Q: When funds are limited, what might the possible benefits be of asking people to take personal responsibility, make judgements, solve problems, be creative, and demonstrate fairness and good sense?

NB: I fervently wanted to ask, "Is the search for a 'fair' **system** now the only agenda?", but immediately recognised it as a 'why' question that would inevitably elicit a defensive and justifying thinking from a lot of respondents. The best questions usually generate a list of possibilities and aspirations.

I want to **stress** that the desirability of high quality questioning is not a justification for professionalisation. It is simply part of thinking. Some people in all walks of life are brilliant at the sort of thinking that makes a difference, gets things done. Most of us are born with the talent and the potential and then, as Ian Chakravorty's vignette graphically demonstrates, get it drummed out of us in early life as those in authority demand our compliance, insist that we follow the procedure, slavishly adhere to the instructions. It is no accident that the best facilitators and innovators are usually rule-breakers and free thinkers, entrepreneurs and anarchists.

Building Relationship Networks

We cannot stress it enough. For the vast majority of us, people and relationships define our lives. And our relationships largely comprise our non-financial/property wealth – our social capital. If our situation excludes us from the social opportunities associated with work, intimate relationships, reciprocal and interdependent interactions with neighbours, congregate or 'team' activities, and so forth we are likely to be socially excluded, lonely, and feel powerless and demoralised. In this state we run the risk of being totally dependent upon funded services. Funded 'care' services, with few exceptions, are not rewarded for discovering or potentiating natural and more rewarding support arrangements, helping reconstruct someone's bank of social capital, nor reducing their client's dependency upon them and, hence, the pounds invoiced.

This is not news. Social exclusion has been on the agenda for a long time, though primarily in the context of community safety, crime reduction and the alienation of disadvantaged young people. Nonetheless, lots of commissioners have had a go at the issue. Unfortunately, instead of putting the challenge where it should be, at the core of social care policy, it has been approached as a bolt-on to the essential business of 'responding to an exponential growth in demand', 'our bread and butter priorities', and 'meeting our statutory responsibilities'. So fixed term project funding has been found to fund the establishment of Circles Networks, PLAN-inspired initiatives, Parents for Inclusion networks, and their derivatives. Then the consequent organisations are usually permitted to wither on the vine as commissioning champions move on, new cool fashions take off, or the playground fairness that it is someone else's turn to scrape the mixing bowl are applied. Then the victim is implicitly blamed for the low impact and coverage of their project. It is evident that it is 'too hard to do this' or that 'people don't relate to these American ideas'.

It is true that in the UK we are disadvantaged by a welfare and service dependent public attitude and language. In Canada, PLAN will not accept government money to establish and support a local organisation. That implies accepting and delivering government agendas and perhaps eventually having no mission of your own. There the members fund and/or raise the funding for their organisations, guard their independence fiercely, and write vetoes against the acceptance of 'funding strands that will become the rope that hangs us' into their constitutions. Sustainability, they have learned, arises from non-dependence on public funds. It will take a long time for most

Brits to take such an independent stance. We are too used to demanding that 'they do...'

A revolutionary opportunity

But, as long as their use is not too negatively delineated, personal budgets offer a real opportunity for lonely and isolated individuals to create a demand for organisations and individuals with the knowledge, skills and connector profiles to respond effectively.

Finding Connectors

We have learned from expensive and bitter experience that not everyone is a 'connector'. Indeed, we found out the hard way that you cannot train people, and in particular social care staff, to function effectively as network facilitators. That is as thankless a task as taking a twenty stone rugby prop forward and training him to win the Olympic High Jump!

They are out there

During the 1990s, whilst I was leading *TACT's* development, we invested heavily in training staff to support people into fully included lifestyles with jobs, friends, social lives and social capital. And we helped quite a lot of people to get these things and they or we were able to tell their stories *pour encourager les autres*. One day, at a small *In Control* seminar in London, I found myself as a 'support act' to John McKnight. As usual our stories hit a chord and went down well but I was aware that John was relating a different lesson. As I remember it he talked about 'glass half-full' and 'glass half-empty' people. On the basis of long research he numbered the large majority of people who entered the caring professions and human services work in general amongst the 'glass half-empty' and dominant personality profile in society. He said people who choose to work in human services:

- Are generally people who want to help others, and especially those who they feel have been dealt a poor hand.
- They see what is wrong and they want to be part of the remedy.
- They tend to see the community as an inhospitable and dangerous place.

- They are often quite disconnected from their own communities with a small coterie of confidantes who frequently share their professional interests depend upon rules and procedures to guide their actions.
- They tend to look towards the professions for solutions to needs and problems.
- And tend to see the worst in people and situations instead of the goodness and opportunities;
- Consequently they are generally risk-averse
- View the folk they are working with as vulnerable;
- And restrict the possibilities and options available to their 'vulnerable' clients to those where they feel they have control or can demonstrate safe and responsible decision-making;
- (I would add that) they are also the people who, if in positions of authority and accountability, initiate inquiries/witch-hunts, identify culprits, and 'tighten up procedures' in response to problems without ever considering that dependence on systems and lack of professional freedom and trust for staff might be the underlying causes of poor performance by staff who began their careers with a social conscience.
- They often find it hard to let go – possibly because they perceive their clients to be incompetent or irresponsible – so tend to review ad infinitum.

This list of characteristics, despite my acerbic intervention, should not be viewed as either negative or critical. Most of the characteristics listed above are ones that I would want to associate with a surgeon as he opens me up, the pilot of my transatlantic flight, a nurse administering dangerous drugs, or a lawyer drafting a vital contract. However, I am less comfortable with it if it is applied to how I pursue the day-to-day matters of my life.

John asserted that we should not expect people with this 'deficit focused' personality profile to be successful in facilitating the inclusion of marginalized people.

He had learned that communities are well served by nature's 'connectors'. The community developer's challenge is to connect with the 'connectors'. John told us how to identify them. He described them as:

o   Gift centred – they see the skills, capacities, talents and good in others.

o   Very well connected in their communities - administratively (with local representatives, public bodies, service leaders), organisationally (with the folk who lead community groups, church organisations, social and sports clubs, local charities and the like), and interpersonally (people just know these folk and engage with them as sources of information and introductions;

they are the people who know someone who can remove the tree stump in your garden or where there's a good martial arts club for your kids to join).

o People who are pretty universally trusted.

o Having a predisposition to see the community as a good place, a safe place, peopled by kind and helpful friends.

o Natural enablers and informers who take the trouble to find out what people want.

o People who let go – it's your issue not theirs – but 'come back again if this idea or introduction doesn't tick the box' is their style.

o Their mantra might be, 'if at first you don't succeed... try something else'.

o You and those who care for you weigh up the risks, if any.

o And (I have noticed that in UK culture) these people are often community organisers as well. They run the local cricket club, organise the carnival or community festival, are volunteer youth workers or luncheon club workers, or are leading lights in the local steam railway restoration. The local shopkeeper often fulfils the role as does the post person and the publican. Whether role creates function or vice versa is perhaps a moot point. I think that McKnight would assert that the personality comes first.

o Also, for balance, connectors have a dark side too. They break rules or, more charitably, they find ways around rules. They can be impulsive and impatient. They are intolerant of bureaucracy. They can be manipulative and divisive – a consequence of being good at people.

When we are recruiting people as network facilitators we find people with these characteristics and then equip them with some training that is designed to build on rather than stifle their gifts. We often find that creative support brokers share the personality characteristics of connectors and so tend to meld network facilitator training elements into all our programmes to support those involved in supporting self-direction.

Where someone providing brokerage support cannot commit the time necessary for the development of a relationship network or is not effective in that role we would recommend, assuming that strengthening the focus person's network of loving and caring relationships is a clearly defined goal, that a connector or network facilitator should be a component of the initial support package. This may be a paid person, working on a self-employed basis from probably no more than 60 hours per annum (circa 5 per month) or a friend or volunteer. We recommend that close family members do not take on this role. It can involve a lot of asking and it is important that people who are invited to participate in a network can decline without feeling coerced by the feeling that a refusal will sully existing relationships.

Training for Network Facilitators...

...is, as has been repeated *ad nauseam*, in all matters relating to self-direction, non-academic, practical and homespun. We set out to provide something of a framework in which the role is pursued, with helpful reference points and a toolbox of ideas and examples. Our experience tells us that on-going coaching is probably more powerful than the formal training but then the foundations laid by the training are also very helpful, as is peer support from other facilitators met during training.

We have drawn heavily on the knowledge and experience of the *PLAN Institute* in Vancouver and then adapted this for appropriate application in our presently welfare state dependent society. We envisage the emergence of family-led community groups in the *PLAN* mould as the groundswell towards self-reliance, interdependency and independent action unfolds in response to changing social and economic conditions. In the meantime our goal is to do all we can to ensure that the scandal of loneliness and isolation is recognised and that 'No-one Alone' is as instantly recognisable as a cause as 'Nothing About Me Without Me'.

As I have said, we assume that the recruitment process has delivered people who are connectors. So we don't set out to ask people to be something else. Instead we help them to be intentional with their talents and to be aware of what they do well.

Network facilitators are the 'producers' of the network not larger than life 'actor managers'. Some connectors are charismatic animateurs and need to intentionally decide to assume a supporting role. In this context we facilitate some consideration of the role in terms of organising responsibilities. What helpful structures and routines can we establish to support the group? When does organisation and systematisation become obstructive or counter-productive? I tend to use Peters and Waterson's concept of 'loose and tight' as a launch pad.

Most of the key activities of Network Facilitation are things that natural connectors do almost unconsciously most days:

o   questioning and listening;
o   mapping existing and past relationship networks – here we teach Judith Snow's approach as a tool for sharing and recording;
o   networking;
o   being hospitable – using hospitality;
o   enabling;

- asking/recruiting.

We set out to make people self-aware of their talents and strategies in these areas, by helping them describe what they do through the medium of exercises and case studies, to share expertise and learn from each other, and we add input to enhance individual repertoires.

One or two of the activities, however, stray into areas that connectors like to avoid. Quite a lot of this relates to the loose/tight debate and is indisputably on the helpful 'tight' side of the debate. While the roots of relationship networks are best nourished by healthy dollops of hospitality and sociability they are established to actively promote the best interests of their focus person. Consequently, they function best when members of the network assume particular roles and responsibilities and when there is a business focus at the heart of their gatherings. In this context the facilitator is the clerk and advisor to the network. Initially, it will be important to encourage the identification and allocation of roles and through to, with the focus person and the network, agree meeting agendas, compile action minutes, progress chase on agreed actions, and maintain communication between meetings. In our training we help facilitators find their inner 'completer-finisher' and, sometimes, celebrate their discovery.

People – Past, Present and Future?

Whether you are engaged in assisting someone to self-direct or to extend their relationship network, one of your starting points will be their relationship history. So often in life our prospects for the future are influenced by our past. And, so valuably, a great deal of our 'social wealth' can be retrieved with a little effort. Past loves, passions, enthusiasms, triumphs and contributions can be an abundant resource. Take Bill, for instance.

He's in his late 80s, widowed 15 years ago, very 'independent', but increasingly frail. His sons and their families live far away, the oldest in Canada. His energetic and loving daughter, Alice, lives 40 miles away and cares for her partner's very frail mother. Nonetheless, she spends every Sunday with her dad - shopping, cleaning, cooking and planning with him. She telephones every morning and evening. She is worried. She has made enquiries, found luncheon clubs and various day centres and clubs but Bill won't go. He tried a couple "that scared me". Alice has persisted and acquired a personal budget for Bill that is sufficient to buy in a bit of daily support, some cleaning, and that is being used creatively to ensure that he gets a good hot meal linked to some company most days. But Bill is clear that his biggest problems are loneliness and boredom.

Bill loves to tell his life history and we have no difficulty in asking questions that stimulate memories. He was a mechanical engineer and served in the Royal Navy during World War 2, then in the merchant marine, before settling down as a maintenance engineer on the railway until retiring 24 years ago. He is passionate about the steam age and has built working steam engines for his own children and grandchildren. Examples of his engineering expertise are displayed around the house. The rail workers had a social club and a group of men who loved steam had formed 'a society'. "We set up a steam railway around Santa's Grotto in *Bon Marche* one year," he tells us. He also tells us about his love of gardening, the chrysanthemums that were his wife's favourites, the fresh vegetables from his allotment, the rosettes won at the annual show, exhibits at the 'Three Counties', and the horticultural society. Then it emerges that he had another passion – angling. He'd been part of the gang at *Billy Lane's*, a tackle shop run by a national angling champion, and been rated as a match angler. He had fished all the big Midlands events and won individual and team medals – they emerged from drawers as he talked.

Armed with this information our job was easy. The railway club still existed and once we found one person who remembered Bill they led us to many others. The allotments were now a housing development but the horticultural society continued to thrive and, while it took some time to find folk who had known him, our first contact immediately asked to meet him. Similarly, the angling shop was long gone but the Anglers Association flourished. "It makes you think," one of the officers told us. "We often get informed about old members who've died and arrange for the Association to be represented at funerals. It would make more sense to look after them while they are still with us!"

The outcome continues to unfold. We arranged for a number of people to have a chat with Bill over a cup of tea and then invited them together for beer and sandwiches. Since then a rota has been organised so that Bill has a visitor at least three days a week – and a couple of retired people who live locally call in most days. He is helping one of his visitors design a working steam model for his grandson and was asked to judge the autumn blooms at a recent horticultural show. The angling association has introduced him to the disabled anglers 'pegs' on their waters and Bill has dusted off his rods a couple of times and rediscovered, as he put it, "The excitement every time the float slides away". Bill wanted company and a chance to belong again. That has happened and in the process his hall and bedroom have benefited from a fresh coat of paint.

The Means – Resources in their fullest sense

While we at *LivesthroughFriends* are enthusiastic proponents of interdependent communities and making maximum use of natural supports we know the value of money and the services they can buy. So, if we are helping folk self-direct it is important that we know about funding sources, their benefits and their perversities.

Our friends at *PLAN* insist that the problem with public money is the strings that come attached to it – so that you are confined to using it in particular ways rather than making the most effective use of it – and that is not confined to local authority social care funds, it applies even more so to sources such as *Supporting People* and the *Independent Living Fund*. Superficially, it is easy to see why the various agencies have their rules and formulas. There's a fixed budget. They need to ensure that their housekeeping is fair and transparent. They want to make certain that the most needy and vulnerable people are served and, the disingenuous escape clause of the public servant, 'it is public money after all!' Yes it is, and I don't like the way that you administer my taxes – but you don't seem to be accountable for that.

The consequence of all this public accountability and a plethora of agencies and funding systems that is just an incomprehensible mess to the uninitiated and incredibly hard to navigate for those of us that claim some knowledge (the criteria change constantly!) is hardly the user-friendly, joined-up arrangement that politicians say they will deliver. There are many occasions when we are advising someone in the context of these parallel funding sources when we would be delighted if they could have just half the money without constraints as to how they use it to meet their needs, other than that they account for how it is applied.

There must be departments of government that don't have budgets specifically set aside for the benefit of people with social care needs, but with the exception of DFID's overseas aid functions that probably don't apply in the UK (there may well be UK provision for refugees!) I cannot think of one. On top of that there are quasi-governmental sources, including the National Lottery, a plethora of charitable foundations and funds including lots of local funds with closely defined objects, and the world of corporate giving. The world of social benefits is just mind-blowing. CPAG produces an updated guide every year and it's a worthwhile investment if you have a significant need for this information. If it is just now and then, do as I do and nurture a friend or two. The internet is also an ocean of information and one or two useful websites are listed at the end of this book.

I, for one, find it a real struggle to stay abreast of all the ever unfolding options in the funding sphere so prefer to nurture people who blossom in this world and use their advice. It is my experience that I am not alone.

However you choose to manage the information overload one thing is certain – you will regularly find yourself bidding (begging) for money and it pays to develop the skills and discipline of writing concise and lucid proposals.

There are loads of books and websites addressing bid writing and I won't assume to better their advice. I cleave to advice I was given a long time ago that works for me:

o   Read their guidance notes and make sure that your request falls within their priorities.

o   Answer their questions clearly and concisely.

o   Provide the evidence, plans, targets, etc. they request.

o   If you think their approach is wrong, keep it to yourself.

o   Don't send lots of supporting evidence – reports, photographs, letters of support.

- Do write a concise (300 words max) covering letter explaining what you are requesting and why, whether or not it is asked for.
- Enclose a stamped, addressed envelope.
- Don't count on one possible funder – apply widely – this is a percentage game.

Breathing life into Community – whose job?

Successful community re-invention or rediscovery will likely require an opposite approach from government to the command and control, planned and managed approach that is the assumed common sense of our time. Indeed, as I unpack and develop my thinking through these pages, I am increasingly sensitive to the dangers and downsides inherent in an over-dependence upon rational, managerial and superficially 'scientific' or 'evidence-based' thinking – especially where those with position power define what constitutes evidence.

Paradoxically (and when we are addressing humanity we seem to be riddled with it) it will take an incredibly passionate, tenacious, determined and coercive government to dismantle the professional bureaucracies that stand in the way of the emergence of 'new' self-reliant and interdependent communities.

The power of the professions has been all too clearly demonstrated by the redefinition of the self-direction and personalisation agenda in social care in the UK. Early versions of the programme in England adopted the language and imagery of the untrammelled marketplace. There would be 'simple and transparent' systems for establishing our financial entitlement; we would have the funds and the power to devise our own solutions; the constraints on our scope for delivering the outcomes to which we aspired would be minimal. By definition we would *need* professional intermediaries a lot less. Not surprisingly the professional managers, accountants, lawyers, social workers, OTs and many others affected took a different view – not maliciously but often very defensively – and fell back upon the almost innate survival instinct of professionals, the one concerned with demonstrating how much you and yours are needed. Long since, the Social Work profession, which presents itself as a helping and enabling vocation, has allowed itself to be very largely redefined as the arbiter of entitlement, of rationing, and the spokesperson for arbitrary, cash-led hardly accountable, defensive and rule-bound bureaucracy.

The escutcheon of this branch of resource management is *fairness*, something that no-one really believes has been achieved, but it is no surprise that the profession should look at the new proposals, generate exceptionally complex assessment processes for the proving of eligibility and Byzantine and secret methods for establishing the extent of financial entitlement, and then argue that people will need their help to 'navigate' the system. I, for one, would favour a very transparent and quick, if rough and ready, benefits system approach with the consequent transfer of resources from process to outcomes.

The profession then goes further to protect its own interests, which includes a clear pecuniary interest, by impugning both the competence and good name of the taxpayers who create public funds. Not content with being arbiters of fairness and entitlement, our former enablers, empowerers and representatives of the oppressed, insist that we need them to police what is going on and to – after all it is 'public money' (like it's sanctified!) – ensure that it is used appropriately and value for money is delivered. Could it be a question of pots and kettles?

Gethin's dad and I campaigned for a long time so that he could have a little bit of money to employ a network facilitator for just 60 hours a year. It took 3 social care department staff visiting together to agree a simple direct payment for just £2k, and that after months of misinformation, meetings and confusion because the organisation could not 'navigate' itself.

Diversity lies at the heart of the *LivesthroughFriends* approach to supporting people to self-direct, and communities will, in our vision, sprout a spectrum of support mechanisms, necessity being the mother of invention, if only the social engineers and power brokers will get out of their way.

The extent to which government wants to influence communities is clear from its own communities website (www.communities.gov.uk). On a page headed, *What is community empowerment*, the opening statement says that, 'Community Empowerment (note the capital letter – it's a programme) is about people and government, working together to make life better'. So, even when it is re-empowering communities, and for me that implies returning or restoring powers that have historically been 'acquired' from individuals and their communities, it is in the context of its agenda. In fact the vision set out by the then Home Secretary David Blunkett went further. It was about 'people taking responsibility for tackling local problems, rather than expecting 'others' (read government) to do so'. So, to paraphrase, 'there are problems in our communities that government is not very good at dealing with and, to be frank, it costs a lot as well. Part of our problem is that we, at all levels of government, are over-systematised, too line-managed, take an age to get decisions made let alone actions taken – whereas you are close to the action, understand what's going down, and can probably come up with some effective solutions. The problem is that the people in local government get their knickers in a twist if they are not seen to be calling the shots on things like this and none of us can get our heads around putting limits on what government can take over like they have in the US. So, what we'd like you to do is do your thing handcuffed to public bodies – you might say with your hands tied behind your back. If you are successful we'll sort of patent your method, write a procedures booklet and back it up with some cool IT systems that take ages to maintain, and employ public servants to roll it all out. Sounds good, yes?'

The other big difficulty for government is to step away from the tools and technologies of management and social engineering. The culture adopted by the over-reaching State and reinforced by the way in which it holds itself accountable to a similarly blinkered media and uninformed populace is based upon detailed, costed plans, targets, timeframes, and statistics. This managed work programme approach is often acceptable when you know most of the variables when you start and initiative, innovation, new relationships and connections, and in-process resourcefulness are not central considerations. It works if you are going to build a house with standard materials from your local builders' merchant off a clear architect's plan, assuming that the ground is stable and the site has been satisfactorily surveyed. It does not work when you dispatch a team of volunteers or enthusiasts into a virgin territory with the permission to build new lives for themselves, with the suggestion that it might be sensible to start off by building some dwellings utilising the resources they find.

During the drafting of this book I have re-read elements of *The Careless Society*, John McKnight's seminal description of the devastation caused to communities by the colonisation of professional services, over and over again. He describes the problem, often signalling the remedies, in 149 pages. He, with John Kretzmann, then provides a summary description of community organising in the US, majoring on the work of Saul Alinsky, in the 1980s in 7 pages. Finally, amidst more criticism of the dominant professional service consumer environment, he describes the attributes of 'communities of associations', 'recommunalization', and locates this in personal faith-based context. This all transpires within 18 pages wherein more than half are taken up with a further analysis of the problem.

In writing this, no criticism of John McKnight's approach is implied. The simple fact, as I see it, is that the 'Regeneration of Communities', is essentially not the stuff of strategic plans, pilot projects, and service constructs. More importantly perhaps, it is not the comfort zone of the systems enthusiasts who dominate public bureaucracies – the people who essentially believe that nothing is valid if it cannot be counted and that the role of people is to deliver 'the plan'.

Fortunately McKnight's analysis has been tested by lots of social entrepreneurs, self-helpers/mutual-aiders, and even public servants – many of whom knew nothing of his research – with great success. The Time Banking movement, Alcoholics Anonymous, the Grameen Bank and micro-finance, Beyond

Welfare (claimants collaborating to break out of the cycle of dependency who are now closely associated with the asset-based approach), and hosts of family-led and inspired groups (like Petagma in Athens) evidence how the world is changed when people recognise the inability of systems and institutions to provide care – the care that is a heartfelt gift given freely from one individual to another. Successful organisations (or more precisely their ideas and intellectual property) that provide stuff that can be easily translated into the framework of services are usually annexed, absorbed, or re-branded by the programmes and services institutions and offered as the latest panacea. If there are no careers to be made or bucks to be banked, systems grounded in self-interested materialism tend to hold them on the periphery.

When Bill Wilson, in response to his own life threatening alcoholism, evolved AA and in the process developed the 12 Step Recovery Model and a culture based upon no ownership, personal responsibility, and interdependency there must have been a terrible temptation, as people from around the world approached him with requests for help in establishing their own 'affiliates', to incorporate the brand, farm personal status and perhaps wealth, and pursue a no doubt rewarding career as a training guru and inspirational speaker. Somehow, it seems that Bill just knew that institutions did not connect with him, demanded a compliance and reverence for expertise that repels people in chaos, and were somehow unwelcoming, devaluing and even rejecting. He understood that people like himself – through relationships, common cause, empathy and often tough caring - had worked his 'salvation'. Gurus, experts, presidents, officers, hierarchies, plans, targets, inputs, outputs and outcomes and all the accoutrements of institutions were not just unnecessary they were contrary to the very soul of AA. I'm not sure that, had he been socialised in our contemporary world, Bill could have stepped back and let go of his great insight as he did. However, I like to think he would have.

At the simplest level the 'How' is just about government, services, and professionals getting out of the way, not cataclysmically but incrementally and very transparently, and recreating a wider awareness of need for interdependent communities. In those circumstances leaders and animateurs and enablers invariably emerge, helping everyone see:

- What they have – individually, as neighbours, and in their place.
- That abundance grows from creating new connections and relationships between ourselves and our assets.
- That good things happen when we individually or collectively act to make the connections – they don't just happen by themselves.
- And that bad things are happening – breakdowns in social cohesion; loneliness and isolation; unsafe, racist

and violent neighbourhoods, etc. – because we have stopped engaging interdependently with our neighbours.

This construct is fraught with problems for contemporary politicians. I can hear John Humphrys or Jeremy Paxman imagining that they are the voice of everyman, stridently haranguing the responsible ministers with cries of, "It's just cuts, isn't it?" Then there will be the spokespeople for the 'charities' and 'independent' service providers who predict horrors for their customers and massive unemployment amongst their employees – despite the fact that there will be significant funds in the system, spent increasingly by people themselves or seeding communities of associations. Concurrently, the machinery of the social care marketplace in local authorities will be screaming 'foul' as the professionals and managers who have been administering the system glimpse the possibility of real redundancy. And all of these forces will inevitably stir up fear and anger amongst consumers.

This is a scenario to cause the most committed enthusiast to consider an alternative career. Perhaps a less confrontational, more iterative, and more educational State strategy is indicated? And, concurrent to unfolding and winning buy-in to a longer term, but still very challenging, vision and evolving strategy, there might be palpable financial and legislative support for individuals and organisations to use their talents and resources creatively in pursuit of the re-invention of interdependent communities.

That being said, public servants from time to time do get exercised about the limitations of agencies in addressing serious community needs and set out to empower and resource people and associations, formal and informal, within communities to generate solutions (NB: not to action the agency's imposed solutions). Asset Based Community Development Trainer, Mike Green in *When People Care Enough to Act* (written with Henry Moore and John McKnight) quotes Mark Twain in describing how politicians and public servants let us all down when they fail to appreciate the tools and resources we have:

'If the only tool you have is a hammer, then the whole world looks like a nail.'

He provides an image of a toolbox with the addition of a saw. The saw - representing people, communities, associations and democracy – is a shaping tool. Imagine, he says, how strange it would be to find a carpenter trying to cut his wood by smashing it with his hammer and asserting that this is the only way of getting the job done. He suggests that the tools of business are not suited to the work of enabling care and interdependency. He recommends that politicians and public servants should be cognisant of and comfortable with both the hammer and the saw and able to pick the right tool for the job.

Green is not, however, presenting an image that implies manipulation by the institutions. The community 'saw' is powered and directed by ordinary citizens. In the same work John McKnight writes:

A genuine partnership is a relationship of equal power between two parties of distinctive interests. Each preserves its authority, distinct capacity and integrity but gains power through the partnership. It is difficult to find many examples of authentic partnerships between systems and associations. Instead, the actual power relationship is most often a system using a community of associations to foster its own ends.

Step one for UK policy makers and implementers is to recognise that this is as a problem, to be aware of it in their own behaviour, and then to commit to act differently. In the same piece, McKnight uses terminology that rings very true in England. Here he talks about three manifestations of 'partnership' between the system and the community – three examples of the imbalance in power and probably unconscious exploitation and control of citizens. He cites **system outreach** where a subsidiary/contractor of the system is located in the community to assure access to local need. 'Voluntarisation' and the encouragement of delivery functions within social care to reconstitute as social enterprises are prime examples of the blurring of the line between the statutory and 'community', the power largely still residing with the 'hammer', as it does increasingly given commissioning and contracting of 'anything that moves'. He also identifies the *citizen advisory* function as characteristic of clienthood not partnership. Here 'representative' citizens are chosen by the system to react the system's plans. Without authority or a real vote and overwhelmed by 'experts' and 'realists' the role is at best advisory and more often tokenistic. Consultation is built into the statutory accountability process in social care in the UK and is largely meaningless. In our work we meet large numbers of people who nominally represent us whose knowledge and beliefs around particular issues reflects the information and opinions presented by the consulting authority. And, more sinister, self advocates who don't because of experiences that suggest that too well-informed criticism or dissidence in respect of plans or interpretations will lead to a re-commissioning of advocacy services. However, McKnight's other misnomer for partnership is identified as *volunteering*. In his definition this amounts to the community being used as a source of unpaid workers by the system. At the time of writing, in England, increasing the numbers of people engaged in volunteering is number 4 on the national performance indicators for local authorities. Perhaps this should be no surprise at a time when public spending is scheduled for unprecedented cuts. However, I would be surprised if loving one's neighbour made the statistics or being active in the local MS Society or sharing the death watch with the wife of a terminally ill work colleague. In short, our policy makers need to get to understand the real nature of communities and society and the very different role that they should be playing in helping self-regulating and self-sustaining interdependent communities emerge.

One who did - in Savannah, Georgia, USA – was Henry Moore: someone, in my view, who contributed far more to the well-being of the world than his far more illustrious artistic namesake. For 17 years he was Assistant City Manager in Savannah, working hard providing services to improve the lives of his communities. "Initially I saw it as my City Hall, my community, my work... any good ideas at all had to be in City Hall, my idea or approved by me," he said, "...I behaved like a Lord when my role was to be a servant." But, despite all the hard work, the desire to do good, the high flown management practice, the comprehensive systems, Savannah, in Henry's word, had, "hit the ceiling". A vicious drug culture established itself in the city and a dependent, deskilled and alienated populace came as consumers to city government insisting that the city should fix the problems, a vortex of vicious circles that saw communities, in all their facets, disintegrate. Henry recognised that he was striving to run both his department and the city in a top down, control and command way – and that in both contexts his behaviour was stifling personal responsibility, creativity and ownership. He came to the conclusion that managers *must lead by stepping back* and measure success *by the extent to which residents take ownership in neighbourhood revitalisation.* He concluded that the City's assets were not a fortress to be closely guarded but a treasure chest available to all. Leading was not about an occasional foray from the fortress, clothed in position power, to 'consult' and earnestly 'listen' before returning behind the battlements (or these days security doors and code-locks) to continue to feed the beast. Instead, leading involved being an equal and responsible partner within the circle with other community leaders. No longer was Henry a leader who would feign empathy, nod sagely, imply a commitment to help and then retire from the firing line to redefine the issues in terms of what the system could do and confirm this in writing. The new Henry and his team were out there on the ground cultivating the connectors and activists who worked in the gap between the system and grassroots communities and through these natural community leaders helping folk agree what was priority for their neighbourhoods and finding ways of putting them in the driving seat as the remedies were implemented. A very simple and inexpensive programme, *Grants for Blocks*, was iconic. Grants of upto $500 were available for any group of neighbours who wanted to do something to improve their living environment. This scheme simply brought people together and threw up community leaders. It was so popular that recognition of the schemes with the greatest impact was regularised as a high profile monthly award. In just a few years citizenship was reborn in Savannah and derelict no-go areas were restored as hospitable and integrated communities, characterised by a caring, well-informed, mutually reliant and assertive populace.

The parallels with UK attempts to realise the fundamental aspirations of inclusion, personalisation and self-direction are, for me, all too clear. We will not, except by blurring our vision and redefining our criteria for success (a process that never ceases amongst policy makers and interpreters I'm afraid), secure a 'National Care Service' without the full and unmanipulated involvement of citizens (not customers!). The 'National Programmes and Services Service' will be what we get unless we change our style of public administration and service delivery and work as equals with our funders – ourselves, citizens, and our associations. Put graphically those of us who live by the hammer need to add the saw to our toolbox. Those of us with the power need to take responsibility for redistributing it amongst those who can use it more effectively; and take responsibility for empowering others. This, in particular, applies to politicians who would be well advised to discontinue their preoccupation with micro-managing and populist reaction and think about visioning, leadership and their commitment to democracy.

The public and charitable foundation funding of grassroots community development presently is almost universally compromised by application and decision-making procedures that require detailed plans about how organisations will achieve their objectives linked to requirements that they meet the requirements of approved providers within the social care market. It might be a good start for government to let it be widely known that it considers the application of competitive and 'professionalised' service procurement practices to the funding of community/self help organisations and community development initiatives to be perverse and counter-productive practice. It seems that service commissioners are yet another 'profession' to cloak themselves in unintelligible jargon and arcane rituals that only the initiated can perform – its practitioners making themselves indispensable as interpreters and navigators of the craft. I would dispense with them and, having devised a simple and transparent approach to the allocation of affordable public funds (that will continually evolve) to people in need of support, I would let the solutions that people devise shape the service provider market. Concurrently - commissioning of a sort I admit - I would invest in:

- promoting interdependency, self-reliance and mutual aid – building bridges between people with disabilities and their communities;
- animating and nurturing local citizens' organisations, primarily but not only user and carer agencies;
- staying alive to the fact that everyone – including citizens with disabilities - wants and needs to contribute;
- generalising creative thinking and problem solving;
- with particular emphasis upon the development of a culture of can-do, person-centred and community-embedded providers (the sort where the social accounts dominate Board agendas);
- promoting local democracy – encouraging everyone to bring their gifts to be part of the solution, welcoming diversity and contrarianism;
- and in PEOPLE with ideas and the entrepreneurial will and passion to see projects to fruition;
- going further than consulting – stepping back and handing over some of the power and the responsibility.

It can help to recast oneself as the conductor of a wonderful orchestra. All of the players before you play their instrument immeasurably better than you and excel when you enthuse that they express themselves and recognise their contributions. But without your attention to the whole work, to synchronisation, to tempo, to balance and organisation the consequence could be chaos or, at best, a curate's egg. During the performance you may not make a single sound. If you have an unassuming style the audience may hardly notice you. Music is often best appreciated with one's eyes closed.

Social networks make change possible. Social networks are the very immune system of society. Yet for the past 30 years they have been unravelling, leaving atomised, alienated neighbourhoods where ordinary people feel that they are powerless to cope with childbirth, education or parenting without professional help. Risk averse professional practices and targets imposed by government have exacerbated the trend...

The core economy operates an economy of abundance. Market prices value what is scarce and so will always overlook our abilities to love, care, mentor, tackle injustice, and all the other things that make us human...

Public service reform models that fail to value it and help it flourish, instead relying more on price signals and narrow legal contracts of service delivery, are themselves part of the problem.

'Co-production – A manifesto for growing the core economy.'
New Economics Foundation.

The lucky dip

Gifts from friends

Bringing It All Back Home
Letter to a Board member

Dear Board member,

There is a problem with organisations.

Being prepared to make major changes is what most executives will not do or are not prepared to do. Certainly this is true of corporate Boards. Look at their makeup: twelve people who are in other businesses and who have other lives to live. Why would they
want to create havoc? So they'll make cautious instead of intrepid decisions. Boards are set up to be conservative; they're anthropological pillars.

Ricardo Semler, the revolutionary 'Anti-CEO' of *Semco*, spells out a major challenge you face in giving people who need support their lives back. For there is a whole industry out there, full of organisations like the ones he describes who have, at their deepest, secret heart, survival first and then growth. You will know this. You are part of one.

You have to be business minded to survive. But how does helping someone to be more independent equate with, say, the imperative to increase market share? You need more support hours, not less. How does someone's desire to spend an evening alone fit with industry's contractual obligations to its staff? Because the industry is a big employer, the needs of people often come below the needs of staff.

Of course, you will probably find a way to risk assess it so that our person does not get to be alone anyway. The industry is constantly afraid it will be sued. You and your colleagues are usually business people steeped in the art of making money – hell some of you are even bankers. "What if something happened to this person?" you ask. "We must protect ourselves first." And you go home and sleep well that night. Priorities, priorities.

Reclaiming support so people get lives through brokerage, connecting into communities, creating support circles, learning, organising and networking with carers, creating alternative routes that avoid service land and a myriad other means, is now possible, although it is all alien to you. No money in it.

Time you learnt. Keep your interest, but find out what is going on locally and get involved in a circle of support. It's your new 'Board' – a microboard; groups of people with the life of the individual at heart, not the money they represent. Imagine! You can get involved with someone you actually know, not dictate to someone you've never met, who might live at the other end of the country. People who need support do not want to play any more by rules that put a cash value on their heads.

I know you don't really want to exploit people; to make decisions that diminish the lives of people you've never met so the organisation you support can keep growing, like a parasite. That's not what you came into this for.

But now there are alternatives to The Industry; real humans, real community, real life. People still need your help. You aren't doing it sitting up there. Come on down my friend.

Simon Malzer does consultancy and independent support brokerage in Scotland. He co-founded *You Direct* (www.youdirect.org.uk) to offer help with planning and organising support for people, their families and carers and also the organisations that support them. For Simon, being independent means creativity is unfettered. People get lives through authentic choices. *You Direct* helps that to happen.

Specialist in the Ordinary

A specialist in the ordinary is what I aim to be

Slicing my way through the porridge of bureaucracy.

Stamping on policy, and rules that make no sense

Endeavouring to make a difference whilst others sit on the fence.

Shunning the traditional norm and knocking down the walls,

Supporting people to challenge the system and live their lives to the full.

It's not always easy in this social care arena – too many suits and people professing to 'have been there'!

The challenge is to challenge and stick to the principle

That life is no tick box and is never simple

It can't be measured by targets... profit and loss

Only by living it and being your own boss

People need to know that they have the choice

To manage, control and live as they choose

Or risk not having a voice

So a specialist in the ordinary is what I aim to be – helping people realise that this is the best way to be!

Estelle Christmas Aug 09

From Jack Pealer

In 2008 Steven Webster and his family (mom, dad, brother, sister), who live near Cincinnati, Ohio, chose to use PATH to help Steven and his supporters think more clearly about the future. Among other things, the choice to use PATH meant that Steven and his supporters had to consider this question: what do we need to do **to get and stay strong** as we move forward along the PATH?

Because Steven's supporters are scattered literally around the world —his beloved sister lives and works in Australia — they said that they would need a way to stay in touch, to share in the changes in Steven's life, to learn from each other as everyone moved ahead. The PATH session was on a Saturday afternoon at the family's church. By Sunday morning, Steven's brother Andrew had created 'Steven Webster's Yahoo Group'. By Monday, supporters started signing up, exchanging ideas, posting photos and learning more about each other.

As weeks and months passed, group members got to share in Steven's first trip away from his family home without his mom and dad — the Great Cleveland Adventure, when Steven went to visit his aunt, her family and others near 300-miles-away Cleveland. Group members could witness Steven's experience trying out various jobs during his last year of school (he's 22 and just graduated from his local school).

Since it began, Steven's Yahoo Group has attracted 42 members. 244 messages have been posted. 553 photographs — of Steven at work, at home, with his friends, doing things he loves — tell the story of Steven's enthusiasms. Without the pictures and messages who would have guessed that Steven loves to watch heavy machinery at work or that he would be so skilled and patient helping his grandmom make a quilt?

Right now group members are helping Steven discover the kinds of work he'd like to do in the next few years and finding places to do that work. Group members use a calendar on Steven's site to mesh their schedules with Steven's — finding the right times to get together with him. Somewhat later, the group may work with Steven to establish a home of his own with people he cares about. The group's energy is sustained, in part, by its decision at the outset that members should stay in touch, with each other and with Steven. The Yahoo Group has supported such togetherness.

Steven doesn't 'self-direct' the funds for his supports right now, but that's likely to happen in the future. When it does, his circle of family and friends, who have stayed in contact with each other, will enable him to put support funds to good use. Steven is ready to reach for his own personal heights.

Jack Pealer has spent 39 years in Ohio/USA trying to make formal systems work for people with disabilities and families. He has also learned how to critique those systems, using PASS 3, and to help people re-shape or escape from services through person-centred planning.

Our Place

The world was born fat, not thin
Like a pot-bellied stove.
She glows in the sky of Mars
half draped in fine robes
licking her fingers, after tasting the stars
as we improperly cover her up
and peek through ours

The world was born full, not empty.
Fertile, not futile.
Fermenting wildly,
Not still and cold.
She needs to be all or nothing,
On not off, beautiful and bold
Like sherbet she should surprise
and like snow in july
she should never do what she is told.

The world was born blind,
She does not see black or white
Or class or creed
nor difference
as some 'special need'
she just feels the tug
of each of her children
on that belly, as we feed.

© Bernard Pearson

What if Steve Jobs ran services for people with learning disabilities?

Steve Jobs - the man who founded and runs *Apple* - is a hard man to please.

He is the ultimate hard-driven entrepreneur - a narcissistic over-achiever with the kind of personality that believes he can, literally, change the world by force of his own will.

He is known at *Apple* for asking the impossible - then getting it. The company's phenomenal innovation - which puts the rest of the industry to shame - is widely credited to this man's drive and the ridiculously high standards he sets.

For example, not only does he insist that all *Apple* devices look beautiful on the outside but also on the inside too. Even the sealed units the buyer never sees.

Jobs, however, is no tech-guy. He doesn't understand circuits or programming particularly. He is the ultimate user and his genius seems to be in getting people to produce the kind of gadgets that make us all gasp with awe.

So, onto my main point.

Jobs has made *Apple* into a company that achieves far, far more than should be possible. He works by a mixture of terror, exhortation and the inculcation of the very highest standards.

Is *Apple* a one-off, or could Jobs transform public services for the better?

More specifically, what would he do to services for people with learning disabilities (and, yes, I am going to talk about `services for' because this is what 90-odd percent of people still get in this so-called age of personalization!)?

The parallels, on first impression, feel ludicrous. IPods and day-centres are not the same thing.

But over-achievement? Customer delight? Genius in design?

Services for people with a learning disability could use a bit of this.

Jobs would, of course, have his work cut out. For the learning disability services sector is, by and large, not one into which one would not readily entrust somebody whose future you really cared about.

So what would happen?   Well, I suspect that the complaisant culture of most service-providers would come under massive attack from day one as Jobs sought to inculcate the notion of excellence into organisations for whom 'excellence' meant something you printed to the corporate literature sent out to Commissioners.

He would also champion customers. As the self-styled 'ultimate end user' we'd see Jobs finding clever new ways to enable people and their families to 'turn the dials', not the care companies.

Whichever way, it would be an interesting experiment. One the world would, I am sure, learn something from. And until we receive the public service equivalent of the iPhone, it is something I will call for - however silly it makes me look.

Craig Dearden-Phillips MBE

Craig is founding CEO of *Speaking Up*, a social business and charity which empowers people with learning difficulties, mental ill-health or other disabilities to have a voice and control their own lives. *Speaking Up* delivers a range of services for disabled people including life-coaching and professional advocacy. It funds itself through advocacy contracts with Local Authorities and PCTs, grants and a consultancy, training and publications business.

In 2002, *Speaking Up* was a struggling local voluntary organisation with 20 staff and a turnover of just £500,000. The decision to start trading as a social enterprise allowed them to build up a successful advocacy services business. *Speaking Up* now has a £5.5 million turnover and helps more than 4,000 people a year. It has also won a host of major awards both within the 'Third Sector' and the wider business world, including the National Training Award.

Outside of his work with *Speaking Up*, Craig is a non-executive member of the Investment Committee of *Futurebuilders England* and a Trustee of *Impetus Trust*. Craig Dearden-Phillips is set to deepen his impact on his local area after being elected as a Liberal Democrat County Councillor in Suffolk.

Craig was awarded an MBE for services to social enterprise in the Queen's Birthday Honours 2009.

Let go – Let live

Dominic Lodge

Letting go is hard. It is hard to let go of a loved one or to accept that someone we care for needs to be free, to fly and to be less dependent.

I remember meeting a gentleman with a disability who used an electric wheelchair to get around. Peter lived in residential care and craved to be in his own accommodation. "What is stopping you from achieving this?" I asked. Well, he had been told that there was still a lot to learn, including managing his money, cooking, directing a personal assistant and finally, after seven years of trying, travel training, or in other words being able to get about safely in his wheelchair. I was deeply perplexed. If someone had said to me that I could not leave home until I had learnt to manage my finances well, cook a variety of edible meals and to be able to successfully get from one place to another without getting lost then I would probably be at home still. I left home in order to discover, make mistakes and to learn. It was an act of adult freedom. I entered an adult world where mutuality and vulnerability were possible and I grew to embrace both.

Yet why is it a world of worthiness and merit for the gentleman I met? A hierarchical world whereby someone in a position of perceived power tells you whether you are eligible or not or that you cannot do something because of the need to protect you, make sure you are safe, capable, and experienced.

Thankfully, Peter has moved on beyond the confines of others' need to create a life of dependency designed to corral and contain his life journey. Sure, like us all, there is still something new to learn and discover but now there is an invitation to do so rather than a need to earn permission. Moreover, Peter's supporters see themselves in an auspicious place. It is a place where the act of supporting is framed in a different way. Support is now offered as an act of entrance and exit rather than a place of settlement. There is not a need to hold onto Peter and seduce him into a life of dependency but rather a freedom to let go, to let live. The supporter defines their support in terms of creating possibilities where they, as supporters, may or may not be required any more.

I still hear people telling me that it's tough to let go and that for some of the people we support the journey of less dependency is not for them. Yet surely the very essence of personalisation is that we discern and discover with rather than for. Peter found a life beyond worthiness and merit and continues his journey of interdependence, mutuality and equality with the support of people who understand what he wants. They have 'let go' and now he can live!

From Martin Simon
Director of *Time Banking UK*

> *Mullah Nasrudin was out in the street searching for the key to his house. A friend passing by offered to help him and asked the Mullah whereabouts had he lost the key.*
>
> *"In my house," said the Mullah.*
>
> *"Then why are you looking for it out here?"*
>
> *"Because there's more light out here," replied the Mullah.*

This silly and profound teaching story has been retold for generations to remind us of a common human failing - how we search for answers in familiar (well lit) places.

'Personalisation and Prevention', if these fine concepts are to have any chance of success, will require our public servants to move away from managing services and budgets and to focus on searching out opportunities and incentives for the general public to get involved and be valued co-producers of a modern social care service.

It is only in our local neighbourhoods that they will find all the skills, energy and the relationships needed for effective community-based social care services. Local systems based on mutuality and the pooling of risk (maybe something like the National Health Service that its originators planned) is what I have in mind.

A new mechanism to make it happen

Timebanking is the ideal tool for this broad based community capacity building.

At a time bank everyone is welcomed and valued equally – one hour earns one time credit whatever the skill.

Time credits are 'banked' and people draw on them to 'buy in' the skills of other participants as and when they need them.

A software programme holds a local information system on the skills and needs that people have and when they are available.

Time banking acts well as a 'letter of introduction' for people who are socially isolated and who may only have had contact with professional strangers. We connect people up, share our values with them and off they go, valued members of a social network they can rely on and trust.

Time to give and take

Once in circulation the 'time based currency' takes on a meaning of its own. It is every bit as real to people as the cash in their pockets. However, unlike cash, the time credits reward people for their care, their compassion and their co-operation - and it is recession proof.

You give what you want and get back what you need

The greatest wealth in any community are the skills, experience, local knowledge and connections of people who live there. And time banks have shown that when you ask people to help others in return for the services they receive (and when you truly value their contribution) they will. As the philosophers say - charity wounds.

These days people are well aware that our institutions and financial systems are failing us and that the individualism that has driven society for so long has not brought the universal happiness that was promised.

They understand that our social environment is under threat, just like our physical environment. They all wish the world was a safer and friendlier place to live in and deep down they know that solid relationships and strong communities are the best predictors of well-being.

People want a safe framework, like time banking, to try out another way of being, of belonging; to learn their rights and responsibilities as citizens and to rediscover their capacity for collective change.

Our public services should want to find new ways to nourish the relationships that sustain the informal and priceless exchanges - between extended families, friends, neighbours and the wider community - that are the only source for a social care system capable of reaching everyone.

From Adrian Roper:

Our governments and their servants are forever beset by the challenge to do what the people want (and thereby stay in power) whilst not doing what the people need (which is genuinely to empower them). They are additionally beleaguered by cultural requirements to be, on the one hand, god-like rational planners of evidence-based services, and on the other hand, mere enablers of the 'invisible hand' of the market. The policy and human consequences are all too often random and iniquitous.

Social Care Commissioning

Bread this year was allocated
On the basis of cloud patterns

> *Following the czarina's dream...*

Adrian has 26 years experience of social care in the statutory and voluntary sectors. He is currently the Vice Chair of the Health, Social Care & Well Being Network (hosted by the Wales Council for Voluntary Action) and the Chief Executive Officer of Cartrefi Cymru (www.cartreficymru.org) .

Walkinstown Association building Connections through Community Contribution

By Lorraine McNicholas

To be truly included in our community, we recognise the importance of having a socially valuable role and making a contribution locally. So when we opened our new centre in Inchicore Village (Dublin) we looked for opportunities to build connections and create new roles for ourselves in the community. We contacted our Dublin City Council Community Development Officer, Fran, and asked if he could help us.

Fran suggested that we could get involved in our local community by planting flowers in planters that line the streets of Inchicore village. We decided that this was a great idea. We planted flowers in the planter barrels. The plants need to be watered every day so we use this project as a way of getting to know people in our locality. We go into local businesses and ask them for the water. We always have a chat while we are waiting for the water. People can see us making a contribution to daily life in Inchicore Village and now we know more people in our community. It's all about building connections!

Everyone's very friendly in Inchicore

By Michael O'Byrne

I normally go gardening with Paul and Fintan. We go every day to the planters and water them and if we didn't they would die. The plants don't get any food from the rain so we put food in the water for the plants. But if it is raining we don't go.

I like doing the gardening and I love doing the watering. I meet people in the *Blackhorse* pub. Michael is the man who works in the pub and he gives me water to water the plants and he asks me if I want a cup of coffee. Then the next place I go for water is a shop called *Londis* in Inchicore. Amanda, Sandia, Mary, Tina, Brian and Aaron work there. I say hello to them and they fill the watering can for me. I normally have a chat with them. They are very nice and they are always friendly.

Next I go to the hairdresser and who do I meet? Debbie, Stacey and Stephanie work there. I always ask Debbie for water and she fills up the watering can with me. I have great fun there, they are nice women.

I also go into the *Black Lion* pub and Mary, Cissy & Miriam work there. I have great fun there too. Cissy fills the watering can and then I go outside, cross the road and water the plants. All of the people in Inchicore are always very friendly.

Sometimes people stop and talk to us when we are doing the gardening and they say we are keeping the place nice.

Alan works in the hardware shop. We buy what we need in there. They gave us a trolley to use and we put peat moss and flowers in the trolley because it's too heavy to carry.

Everyone is very friendly in Inchicore!

Left to Right: Michael O'Byrne & Paul O'Rourke

From Tommy Abrams and Lynn Flynn

Tom's Choices

I need new shoes

I want someone to help me find shops that stock my size at a reasonable price

I need to keep my flat clean

I want someone to prompt me to clean up after myself and keep things safe & looking nice

I need help with paying bills & budgeting

I want a budgeting plan to help me save money & someone to check that I have paid my bills on time

I need help with shopping

I want to find bargains

I need to stay healthy

I want someone to remind me about appointments and encourage me to seek medical advice when needed but let me make my own decisions

I need to be occupied

I want to find a hobby and a job

I need company

I want friends and a girlfriend

I need somewhere to live

I want my own house with a wife and children

I need to be safe

I want to learn through taking risks & trying different things

I need to be more confident

I want someone to go out socially with

I need to increase my independence

I want to pass my driving test and own a car or motorbike

I need support, not care

I want people who understand the difference and will help me to achieve my goals

I have been supported by *POTENS* for 9 years, at first in a residential home and for the last 6 years in a supported flat.

I am a keen Everton supporter and karaoke singer and with the support of staff, have just received an award for completing 100 hours voluntary work in a café.

Tommy Abrams

Tommy was supported to compile this piece by Lynn Flynn, Specific Project Manager for *POTENS* who provide support, care & accommodation to people with learning disabilities, mental health issues and physical disabilities.

Lynn has been with the company for 8 years in various roles and is currently involved in the implementation of the personalisation agenda within *POTENS*.

Ian Chakravorty

Go MAD (Make A Difference) Thinking

I want to be an astronaut

I was a maths teacher in the 1990s but the most enjoyable part of my job was the role I had as a form tutor. I really enjoyed working with students on the non-academic side of education. Part of this role was to help students to look at potential future careers and I remember one instance where I believe I got it wrong.

Johnny was 12. He came in one day with a huge smile and told me that he wanted to be an astronaut. It made me smile too and I knew exactly what to do to help him. Using my experience and professional know-how I decided to save Johnny some time and disappointment. I told him that he would never be an astronaut.

He was in low ability sets for most subjects. He was from the local estate that was a bit rough. Growing up on an estate myself as a kid, I knew that the chances of Johnny becoming an astronaut were zero. I gave Johnny the benefit of my experience and gave him some very well intentioned directions – I told him to look at other jobs. I told him to consider jobs that I believed were well within his reach. So he did and the smile left his face.

Johnny never mentioned being an astronaut again.

I think of Johnny often and realise that I did something really bad. Johnny would probably never have become an astronaut. What I did though was stop Johnny discovering what he COULD do. I should have asked Johnny what he needed to do in order to become an astronaut – I think he would have come to his own conclusions... but he might have gone out and bought a book about space or saved up for a telescope and kept his smile. I stopped him looking.

As professionals we do things to help people realise what they are unable to do to save them time and disappointment. I think we all have the right to be disappointed... I also think we have the right to discover disappointment for ourselves every now and then.

Go with the flow and living our life

Penny Papanikolopoulos

Psychologist, Athens Greece

Mihaly Csikszentmihalyi (1997) in the *Psychology of Engagement and Flow* explains that we can all participate in positive 'flow' experiences. 'Flow' is experienced when a person engages in a pastime or occupation that he/she deeply enjoys for even the fewest moments. During these moments, deep emotional and cognitive harmony is experienced such that all difficulties are forgotten and oneness is experienced.

In order for 'flow' to occur, the demands of our pastime or occupation must be slightly above our current level of functioning. It must be a tiny challenge that demands our full attention. When our concentration and attention is focused, then all worry, dysphoria and discomfort is overcome for those few moments of 'flow' with the positive experience of applying oneself to a creative endeavour. We lose ourselves in the work and enter into the very thing that we focus on. The only prerequisite is to be able to focus for at least a few moments.

No matter what social economic group we find ourselves in, life has the same basic elements whether we are a Greek shepherd on a mountain or a Greek tycoon ship-owner. All humans have four major parts to their day: 1) Productive work or learning, 2) Maintenance of everyday life (hygiene, cooking, eating, arranging environment), 3) Leisure time and 4) Sleep and renewal of energy.

The quality of our lives depends on the quality of our emotions and thoughts concerning our work and/or pastime. How do we perceive and how do we feel about the experience of living? Do I focus and lose myself even for the shortest amounts of time, during my pastime? Losing oneself does not have to be a solitary endeavour. One can lose oneself in a wonderful conversation, dance or sport as long as focus is achieved for some moments. Life has an unknown expiration date and we give quality to our lives.

According to Daniel Siegel and his theses on *Interpersonal Neurobiology* (2007) all human behaviour can be conceptualized on a spectrum of chaos to rigidity. Human consciousness develops between the triad of brain, mind and relationships. Brain – body is our mechanism for running our central nervous system while our mind is responsible for regulating and adjusting energy and information both within each individual and between two or more individuals. Mind is the embodied relationship which regulates information and energy. Focus is the prerequisite for changing my experience of everyday life and 'flow'. All humans move on a spectrum between chaos and rigidity in the realm of thought, emotion, image, senses and body experience. Harmony between chaos and rigidity is the goal for quality living.

When working and supporting other humans we commonly face many challenges. Such challenges can be an underdeveloped or traumatized brain-body mechanism and mind adjuster with difficulties concentrating and attending with focus and intent to particular elements of the environment. Many times these difficulties affect execution of gross and fine motor skills, limitations within the realm of abstract thought and production of fantasy. In terms of relationships to self and others many difficulties with social relationships and identification with the disabled part of self. Are the roles that they have valued in their community? Will the person acquire a creative pastime or occupation?

All Learning, therapy and growth require the integration of differential parts into a more harmonious output. Through focus and attention one can learn to integrate the different parts of the mind so that a more unified form of behaviour and experience can occur. 'Neurons that fire together, wire together' (Siegel, 2009), therefore all learning and therapy must stimulate the brain, mind, intrapersonal and interpersonal relationship. The goal is flexible, adjusted, coherent, energized and stable integration of differing parts of self in order to experience even the least amount of 'flow' in everyday life.

Helping others or helping self is one and the same. All humans are in the same lovely predicament called life.

From Dr Andy McDonnell

Challenging behaviours: Back to the basics

I have spent over 20 years of my working life supporting individuals who challenge services. As a clinical psychologist I have always been acutely aware that there has been a growing move towards a mechanistic approach to managing these difficulties. It also took me a considerable period of time to realise that professionals can be part of the problem. They often make complex solutions to difficulties that do not require these as such. I will write this short article from the essential premise that we need to concentrate on what was colloquially described as 'the basics'.

In the mid 1980s I was a newly qualified clinical psychologist, trained in behaviour analysis; I even possessed a briefcase for a short period of time. (I should stress that this was a necessary part of the unofficial uniform at the time.) To complete my rite of passage I wrote an article on functional analysis! This was a very cerebral piece of work which I believe very few people took the trouble to read. But, my first real lesson in 'the basics' came within the first year. I was working in a house for a number of people who had been resettled into the community from a local institution. It is no surprise that many of these individuals were labelled as very challenging. Years of control by well intentioned carers had led to the few pleasures in their daily lives (food and drink) being restricted. Many of these people had extremely traumatic histories (depravation and loneliness being major causes). It was not surprising to me that food and drink was a major behavioural issue. I remember when one staff member complained that every time she 'unlocked' the kitchen door service users would almost charge past her. One young man even accessed a freezer and attempted to eat frozen meat.

I realised very early on that the staff wanted me to 'sort these problems'. Was it all about ABC charts and functional assessment? Or should I attempt to understand the person by thinking carefully about the person's life. The latter started to make more sense to me. People with an intellectual disability who lived in large communal settings probably would have become obsessed with food. This to me reflected a state of obvious depravation of basic everyday pleasures. I then started to ask myself a basic question. *What would it be like to be this person?* The first basic rule was to spend time 'being' with the person and try to 'walk in their shoes'. I did not reject all aspects of behaviour analysis; I merely placed it in a compartment. Since this time I have met many gifted behaviour analysts who apply Positive Behaviour Supports in a systematic and rather mechanistic manner. I think that there can be too much analysis at a distance and not enough time spent directly with individuals developing a basic understanding of the world.

My second basic rule evolved very early on in my career. It became more apparent to me that the people I was supposed to support tended to be placed in 'analytic goldfish bowls'. Carers often were a cause of many episodes of challenging behaviour (mostly inadvertently). Most of my information came from information written by these very same people. Often the most negatively vocal individuals had poor relationships with the service user in question. In many cases these people had real difficulties in taking the service user perspective. So my second basic rule was *'view staff as sometimes part of the problem'*. This could be reframed very easily in a positive manner, if carers can be part of the problem they can also be part of the solution.

The third learning experience for me was that communal care is not for everyone. So many times I would be asked to fix behavioural difficulties and tried to ignore the fact that these individuals often lived with individuals with similar difficulties. As an analogy, if you have a problem with your weight, will you learn to control your weight living with other people with similar problems? Putting it more bluntly, do distressed people improve by living with others who are similarly distressed? I still witnessed traumatised individuals herded together with other people with issues. My third rule involves understanding that crowded environments do not lead to individual supports.

People who have their own supported areas and ideally their own front door have fewer difficulties.

The use of drugs to control behaviour is still at epidemic levels, even though the evidence for their use is very scant indeed. One of my basics rules is that we cannot support people who challenge and ignore the over-medication of this population. For me the rule is clear cut, drugs administered to individuals are often requested by stressed carers. So let us teach these individuals to make fewer of these negative requests. I consider if I would find it acceptable to be placed on medication, even if I was angry or agitated on a weekly basis. For me the answer is a clear 'no'. *In sum, let us make medication the exception rather than the rule.*

In the last 10 years I have worked with many individuals who are supported by large staff teams. In the bad old days of the institutions these were referred to as 'specials'. I always respect the view that people need to be kept safe, but I do feel very strongly that this approach to safety does not empower service users. In addition, these types of services can reduce staff confidence and in more serious situations reduces carers ability to take risks. That is, they feel that they need this level of support to take risks. My last golden rule involves the development of risk taking cultures. The mantra *'take a risk every day'* is my repetitive advice. We learn through experience. A good term from cognitive psychology is 'crystal ball gazing'. Staff teams will sometimes develop a culture where they resist risk taking. When a new activity is suggested it is usually followed by armchair predictions from staff. That is 'I think that would not work' or 'bad things will happen if we try X or Y'.

Cultures that support people in a person-centred way develop a positive attitude to crisis management. There is an acceptance that crises will happen from time to time. Understanding the reasons for these crises is part of the learning process. Despite what we think, things do not happen completely 'out of the blue'. Even if we understand why the individual behaves in the way he or she does we may not be able to prevent all incidents of challenging behaviours. In these circumstances people need to *ride out the storm.* This can be scary for people and practical support is often required. But the storm analogy is clear. We cannot change bad weather but we can learn to adapt to it.

Even when we ride out storms it is useful to remember that the people we support often have histories of abuse and trauma. My colleague David Pitonyak provides useful insights into trauma. It is important to understand that *if we view someone as traumatised it should influence how we manage support them.*

Throughout my career I have been involved in the development of a low arousal approach. This involves a low key response from carers to manage challenging behaviours. In essence it can be reduced to one very basic idea. *Be tolerant and respectful of the person and avoid punitive responses.* This is an easy principle to state but very difficult to apply in practice. I am often reminded of the old saying 'you can take a horse to water, but you cannot make it drink'. I believe passionately that our job is to support and empower people and this involves self-reflection, understanding and tolerance. It is not about 'us' it is about 'them'.

Recap of the basic rules

What would it be like to be this person?

View staff as sometimes part of the problem and the solution

Let us make medication the exception rather than the rule.

People who have their own supported areas and ideally their own front door have fewer difficulties

Take a risk every day

Ride out storms

If we view someone as traumatised, it should influence how we manage support them.

Be tolerant and respectful of the person and avoid punitive responses.

Andrew McDonnell,

Director of Studio3

July 2008.

Why Contribute?

By Lorraine McNicholas, Community Inclusion, Walkinstown Association.

Our contribution to society largely defines our identity. When we meet someone for the first time we normally ask, "What do you do?" We ask this question because it helps us identify with the person. The answer helps us to connect with each other. We naturally expect people to have some type of role or make a contribution to society.

When we contribute to society we strengthen our position in life. We are rewarded for our contribution - we receive wages, acknowledgement, recognition, status, friendship, respect, social connections, health benefits, respect and self-esteem. By not making an active contribution we forgo many of these benefits. However, it is important to recognise that this contribution does not translate exclusively as 'paid employment', it means making a difference in the community with skill and connecting with others. The contribution is not always focused on the monetary gain; instead it may be helpful to consider the contribution in terms of active citizenship. Maslow proposed that as humans our natural drive is to become something more, to create and to contribute. When this creative part of the person is not attended to, people lose touch with their soul, with the essence of what it is to be a person. (Etmanksi, 2004)

Society expects us to contribute. As citizens we are expected to vote, pay taxes and make voluntary contributions. We invest in the social bank, society keeps track of our contribution and we are treated accordingly. The government will establish 'special services' in times of boom but will be very quick to cut these same services in times of recession. We need to ask ourselves, "Are governmental responses guided by their perception of the level of contribution to society by people with disabilities?" Does lack of contribution equal unworthiness? (As suggested by the *New Unworthiness Equation*, Etmanski (2004))

By empowering people with intellectual disabilities to contribute to their community, they move towards a stronger position of citizenship in society. They become 'seen' in the community less as a 'person with a disability' and more as an 'active citizen'. As citizens rather than 'service users' people command greater equality and are therefore treated accordingly. We look forward to a day when we see greater contribution by all citizens to their communities.

References - Etmaski, A. (2004) *A Good Life*. Orwell Cove: Vancouver, Canada.

A Good Life – Developing Local Area Coordination in the North East of England

Ralph Broad

What is 'a good life'? A good life is something that is personal and individual for each person. However, for many people it will include things like:

- love, friendship and a range of relationships;

- a family life;

- a job;

- making practical; choices and decisions

- using and developing personal skills and attributes;

- having control over your life;

- planning and having confidence in the future;

- being a member of your local community and contributing to your community.

Inclusion North, a not for profit membership organisation that works to promote the inclusion of people with learning disabilities, their families and carers in the North East, Yorkshire and Humber, has recently also been leading in the development of Local Area Coordination (LAC) in the region.

LAC is an approach to supporting people with a disability and their families to have 'a good life' that is individual to them, rather than asking, "What services do they need?" It also works to make services more personal, accountable and accessible. It is about helping people to stay strong, rather than waiting for them to fall into crisis and then waiting for resources.

It was first developed by the Disability Services Commission in Western Australia and is now working across many Australian states, Scotland, Canada, Ireland and New Zealand.

What Does a Local Area Coordinator Do?

An LAC works as a single, accessible point of contact in a defined local area, supporting between 50-60 individuals (children and adults) and their families in the local community. LACs:

- get to know people, their gifts, strengths, aspirations and the local communities in which they live;
- provide, and support access to, accurate and timely information from a variety of sources;
- support people to 'be heard' through promoting self-advocacy, advocating with people and accessing local advocacy services;
- contribute to building welcoming, inclusive communities, identifying community opportunities and responding to gaps in local communities;

- assist people to develop personal and community networks to enable practical responses to life needs and aspirations;
- support people to have control of decision making, life choices and resources or funding;
- support people to access specialist supports and services.

What does it achieve?

LAC has been reviewed many times over the past 20 years (see Government of Western Australia, 2003; Chenoweth and Stehlik, 2003 and Scottish Executive, 2007), focusing on outcomes for individuals and their families/carers:

- greater peace of mind and increased security for individuals and families, high levels of satisfaction and increased personal networks;
- increased optimism about the future;
- improved functioning and well-being;
- increasing independence, self-sufficiency and community contribution;
- improved access to information, more choice and control of resources;
- a more diverse and customised array of informal and formal support to meet their needs.

People and families highly value the 'personal relationship, practical support to make things happen in the local community and positive approaches' (Bartnik, 2007).

Parent's comments (Disability Services Commission, 2005)

"I could boil it down in a couple of words: Basically he's on our side. He doesn't question what we say; he doesn't question the validity of my son's opinions on anything. He's there for him and he's the only one who's there for him. He's not on the school's side, the council's side, he's not on anyone's but my child's side; he's there for him."

What Happens Next?

Inclusion North is working with *In Control* and North East local authorities to prepare the development and implementation of LAC as part of personalising services and supports and transforming social care. Middlesbrough is the first authority in the area to start, with 3 LACs planned in one local area in January 2010. Watch this space!

RALPH BROAD

Ralph has 25 years experience in working alongside people with disabilities, their families and their local communities. His passion is in working in partnership with people to support them to get the life they want (a 'good life'), enable contribution, share gifts and promote welcoming and inclusive communities and with organisations to think of more natural ways for this to happen.

He is currently working in partnership with *Inclusion North* and NE authorities to develop a range of approaches to personalisation (supporting people to get the life they want – imagining a better future) and co-production (real partnerships), including Local Area Coordination and Microboards. Local Area Coordination is an approach to supporting people and their families to have a 'good life' as part of their local community and to support communities to include and welcome people with disabilities as valued citizens.

Prior to this, Ralph has worked alongside people and families in 'not for profit' provider organisations, and the statutory sector in roles ranging from direct support through senior director roles in England, Scotland and Australia.

He studied at the Tizard Centre, University of Kent at Canterbury, completing his MA in Management in Community Care in 2007.

Who Cares?

from Colin Campbell, Co-Director, LivesthroughFriends CIC

Ricky is 36 years old. He has Down's Syndrome, a learning disability, and was given the label of 'challenging' after a road traffic accident in which he suffered multiple injuries. At that time he was living with his father and stepmother in a small town in a rural English county. That was 15 years ago. Ricky was due to emigrate with his family when the accident happened and because Ricky was now beginning to be 'challenging' he was sectioned and placed in a secure residential home isolated from the community he grew up in. His father emigrated, leaving Ricky in the residential home. By all accounts this decision was not taken lightly by his father, who took advice from the professionals who were now 'caring' for Ricky. There appeared, according to records, to be a consensus that Ricky did not want to emigrate to the other side of the world. Over the next fifteen years Ricky endured life within this residential home and although very 'challenging' (again, the records state) at the beginning of his stay he eventually 'settled down' into a routine in his new home.

I met Ricky when there was a safeguarding concern around money going missing from the accounts of people who were residents of the home. During my initial visits Ricky was in his room by himself, looking at books, playing CDs and watching DVDs on his TV. I was told that Ricky had a varied timetable and his 'behaviours' were now managed, "Although sometimes you have to be very careful how you manage him and he definitely requires two members of staff when going out in the community: and by the way, we still don't get funding for this". When I asked about Ricky's passions and the people in his life, the reply was, "We will find out and get back to you". They eventually did get back to me with a printed timetable and a list of two people, one of whom did not have any contact details. Over the next few months I spent some time with Ricky, seeing him outside the residential home in coffee shops, out and about in his local town. The first thing I noticed was that people knew Ricky. In the coffee shop Ricky would say hello to a lot of people and some would say, "Hello Ricky, I haven't seen you for a long time – where are you living now?" I spoke to some of these people and began to build a picture of Ricky's life when he lived in the town and found out about some of the people who, in the past, had known Ricky quite well. One of those people was someone who had given respite support to Ricky when he was younger. It then became apparent that she had kept in touch with Ricky over the years by including him in special occasions, birthdays, Christmas etc. She had a friendship with Ricky that was difficult to sustain and nurture because of the distance from her own home and the perceived barriers of the residential home. Interestingly, this was described to me in very non-specific ways by statements like, "They never passed on information" or "There were always different staff on duty and nobody seemed to know what Ricky was doing" and "Of course we can't tell you as it is confidential". Fundamentally, Ricky's friends didn't feel welcome.

Ricky told me quite early on in my contact with him that he wanted to move back to the town where he grew up. So to begin helping Ricky, I established the beginnings of a network with the people who were identified by my initial contacts. Quickly, after only a couple of network meetings with Ricky and his very welcoming friends, a new local contact emerged via relatives from the other side of the world. Ricky's sister lived locally, but a mixture of not feeling welcome at the residential home and the commitments associated with bringing up her own children had led to her losing regular contact with Ricky. However, when I explained that Ricky was looking to move back to a home of his own and there was a fledgling network being developed to support Ricky with getting his life back on track, she jumped at the chance to be part of his life again. Now we have a network of people who had known Ricky in the past including friends from school, his sister and two nephews! At the first network get-together it was a delight to hear the stories of Ricky's life prior to him going into the residential home: it brought alive Ricky's past life and set the scene for his future. In the space of a few months Ricky is now planning a new life with friends and family and nobody has mentioned 'challenging behaviour'!

It has become clear to me, after 25 years' living and working within a system that has professionalised care, that one of the most important aspects of peoples' lives is having relationships with people who know and love them and really care about their welfare, future and the quality of their life. I have also learnt that for many people who have a label of 'learning disability', 'mental illness', 'challenging behaviour' etc. you cannot leave the development of these relationships to chance. It's not negotiable when arranging 'care' for someone that positive relationships are not taken into account and then facilitated in some way. As one member of Ricky's network said at the first gathering when talking about the past 15 years, "Nobody seems to understand – you can't buy care, it's something that is shared between two or more people who really, really know each other".

Colin Campbell - February 2010

Colin Campbell is Co-Director of *LivesthroughFriends CIC* and a network builder *par excellence*. (Bob)

Other Recommended Reading

Orbiting the Giant Hairball – A Corporate Fool's Guide to Surviving with Grace

Gordon McKenzie

(Viking – Penguin Putnam)

ISBN: 0-670-87983-5

The Social Entrepreneur – Making Communities Work

(Atlantic – Business)

Andrew Mawson

ISBN: 978-1-84354-661-0

Maverick!   Ricardo Semler

(Random House)

ISBN: 0-7126-7886-7

Go MAD – The Art of Making a Difference

Andy Gilbert

(Go Mad Books)   Tel: 01509 891313

Amazon have it!

ABCD in Action – When People Care Enough to Act

Green, Moore, O'Brien & McKnight

(Inclusion Press)

 ISBN – 10: 1-895418-74 -7

The Fred Factor   Mark Sanborn

(Random House)

ISBN: 1-844-13816-X

Social Enterprise in Anytown   John Pearce

Calouste Gulbenkian Foundation

ISBN: 09903319-97-7

The Careless Society – Community and its Counterfeits

John McKnight

Basic Books

ISBN: 13-978-0-465-09126-3

Getting to Maybe... How the World is Changed

Frances Westley et al

(Vintage Canada at Random House)

ISBN: 9780679314448

Keys to Citizenship   Simon Duffy

(Paradigm)

ISBN: 0-9543068-2-1

Co-Production and Personalisation in Social Care

Susan Hunter & Pete Richie   (Jessica Kingsley)

ISBN: 978-1-84310-558-9

The Starfish and the Spider

Ori Brafman and Rod A Beckstrom   (Portfolio)

ISBN: 1-59184-143-7

Co-production: A Manifesto for growing the core economy

Download from NEF at www.neweconomics.org

And Helpful and Inspirational websites

www.abcdinstitute.org

www.plan.ca

www.nationalbrokeragenetwork.org.uk

www.timebanking.org.uk

www.mike-green.org

www.gomadthinking.com

www.beyondwelfare.org

www.neighbours-inc.com

www.in-control.org.uk

www.equalfutures.org.uk

www.realife.org

www.neweconomics.org

www.nurturedevelopment.ie

and, of course, www.livesthroughfriends.org

Reinventing Interdependent Communities
A Checklist for Policy Thinkers and Makers

⚓ The Social Care "Crunch" –
The Perversity of Marketization

It seems to me that it is self-evident that communities, rather than commerce, have been the backbone of society since the dawn of human-kind. The notion that we can, in just a few short years, replace the care and interdependence that has been central to our species' survival with an economic activity seems as brash and adolescent an assumption as the assertion that we can, in a blink of an eye, massively over-populate the planet and indiscriminately harvest all aspects of its finite resources without consequences.

At a time when the future funding of social care is bound to suffer from the implications of global warming, the global redistribution of economic clout, the exposure and long term consequences of untrammelled capitalism in the form of the banking scandal, the demographic impact of the post-war baby boom, and increased longevity we are going to need each other more and more.

Hopefully you are persuaded that we need to frame our thinking and our questions about the State's involvement in how we care for each other very differently? Here are a few suggestions for you to consider. They are nothing more – no golden bullets.

In compiling the list I tried really hard to set things out in priority order or as a rational critical path. I couldn't. Assuming a change of mindset, an acceptance and enthusiasm for the perception that we are interdependent social beings who need to be interdependent and social in order to have meaning and security in our lives, then all the other ideas are themselves interdependent and, in a change management context, would need to be addressed simultaneously.

In addressing these issues I would venture that we might start by:

⬇ ASKING A DIFFERENT QUESTION – instead of asking, "what services and benefits should the State provide?", we could ask,

"What sort of society do we want?"

⬇ A CHANGE OF MINDSET – TRUST and GIFTS!

- Servant Leadership – think about your motives and vision.
- If you have one, revisit your vision from the perspective of 'everyman'.
- In particular revisit your vision in the context of individuals, families, neighbourhoods, communities, and UK society.
- Resolve to build and nurture more than to command and control.
- Hold contributing citizenship, the need for relationships and belonging, personal rights and responsibilities, self-reliance, and personal autonomy as central tenets from which to consider social policy.
- View people and communities as 'the talent'.
- Acknowledge everybody's need to give and share their gifts and talents.
- When addressing a need, focus on their gifts and assets and do not 'occupy' their issue – assist them to devise and implement their solution.
- In ensuring the availability of services concentrate on the things that require hard won knowledge and skills, do not deskill and diminish communities, and cannot be done better by our friends – *I value my plumber when it comes to extending my central heating system but I don't need him to run my bath; and, like John McKnight, I view the emergence of the bereavement counselling industry as both an occupation and dehumanisation of previously interdependent and exceptionally sensitive and resourceful communities. When we are down we need love and care and to feel that, in due course, we will reciprocate.*

- See the job as about producing a culture, a good society, a great place to be – somewhere to belong.
- Understand that we are on a journey and that our best efforts never do justice to our vision. Be clear that 'we' is a direct consequence of belonging and having the right and responsibility to contribute, and a great outcome. 'They' is a consequence of exclusion and alienation and a consequence of 'cabinet' decision making.
- Whenever you are tempted to (according to your place in the bureaucracy) legislate, regulate, issue directives (dressed up as guidance), establish another quango or inspectorate, systematise, regularise, use the word 'fair', or in any other way seek to achieve compliance by coercive means, could you take a deep breath, resist the urge and ask yourself and others if there could be a more progressive and societally enhancing way to address the issue in hand?
- And before you say it, I know, I am redefining the role of government and those who aspire to serve, represent and govern. It is in my view long overdue – in a supranational, globalised world we need to 'go local' and encourage participative democracy, self-reliance and cooperation.

⬇ TAKE A LONG VIEW – DO POLITICS NOT POPULISM

- It seems that our electoral system and our adolescent fourth estate contribute to a hegemony focused on now that asserts little or no responsibility for the future. Too frequently it seems that real debate about long term issues are recast as 'disaster movies' for political capital, viewing statistics, or boosted circulation. Our generation is simply a very temporary steward, not only of the planet but also the potential for good in mankind. It behoves those who would represent others to have a stance on these issues and those who are represented to check that actions reflect the oratory.
- In social policy it strikes me that it is only possible to take the long view if we stop reacting and, instead, elicit a broadly shared vision of our world as we would wish it to be. Our shameful history in respect of serious child abuse scandals over the past 40 years is, it seems to me, a simple case of, "if you

always do what you've always done you'll always get what you always got" – that being more bureaucracy, more social policing agencies, more systems, more people to blame, and more wasted public money to little or no effect. Meanwhile we did little or nothing to change the culture that gives rise to the problem. As usual we were led to expect 'decisive' government action and systems to be put in place to ensure that this would not happen again. The press bayed for culprits and politicians responded to the 'justifiable public anger'. Concurrently, over four decades, we have allowed the youth service to wither, education to be recast as qualifications rather than socialisation, made marginalised people increasingly welfare dependent and unself-reliant, allowed our communities to be occupied by professionals and services, recast ordinary life in the contexts of markets and services, and redefined loving our neighbours as volunteering!

✦ **DEVELOP A PERSON-CENTRED VISION** - When you take the trouble to ask people what really matters to them, what is necessary for them to have a good life, it is clear that we all share common priorities and, in the main, they are not the things that politicians and policy makers assume that people want. Put simply, it seems that if you ask people what politicians can do for you, people frame their answers to match their appreciation of what politicians are interested in or feel capable of doing. People now seem to believe that politics is about money, services and management rather than vision, leadership, and principles. The pursuit of happiness might be considered a pretty woolly and unmeasurable goal. However, when folk are asked what really matters they chorus the same consistent group of criteria:

- Loving and caring relationships – a deep sense of belonging.
- Enough wealth to be able to exercise some choice in life decisions.
- The chance to contribute, to earn respect and the rights and responsibilities of citizenship – to make a difference.

- A place or home of my own where I can be and express myself.
- The safety and security derived from the previous four essential elements of a good life.

It is salutary that safety is not seen as being secured by criminal records checks, complaints procedures, inspection bodies, nor, more surprisingly, our well-founded police service. If we want disabled and/or older people or children at risk to feel safe and secure we need to attend to different things to services – like family life, community life, making the most of peoples' talents and communities' assets, ensuring affordable and appropriate housing, and viewing everyone as a contributor.

⚓ WHILE BEING PERSON-CENTRED BE 'SOCIETY-CENTRED' TOO!

It is a beautiful and elegant paradox. As much as we are all unique individuals we are only fulfilled through each other, in relationships, families, groups, clubs, associations, causes, congregations, choirs, teams, and so on.

A response to the human condition that fails to appreciate this is essentially misdirected. For more than three decades it has been assumed that business has the answers and that if human services ape business we will all benefit. This conviction was born out of a market driven political philosophy that saw all public services as flabby, undisciplined and unscientific, and it probably had some validity in terms of many 'concrete' activities like refuse collection or highways. However, it was a conviction born out of ignorance and prejudice when applied to social services. Indeed, the practice of community and social work is far more an art than a science or system - an art that, when practised expertly, utilises the full palette of communal resources and secures inclusion and belonging rather than exclusion and redundancy.

Enabling people to self-direct need not be just about removing the middleman from a shopping expedition. The real potential of self-direction is liberated if we attend strategically to ending the professional occupation of territories where kindness and interdependency should flourish, and supporting citizens to look to each other for those things that, with the best will in the world, services and professionals can't and don't provide.

We simply need to ask ourselves what we can do to assist folk to find joy in giving their gifts and helping each other. As often as not the answer is, **"step aside"**. The second most important answer is, "back the organisers who are taking a lead" and please don't tell them how to do it! Nurture, back, coach, fund but don't direct or claim too much special knowledge or expertise – and don't assert responsibility for things that really are not your business. But first, you are going to have to think about how you can persuade people that they aren't hopeless and giftless, that they can help each other through trauma and bereavement, that there is more to them than being trained rats exchanging more and more labour for isolation and instantly obsolescent toys, that there's much more to life than goods and services – and that that is people, relationships, meaning and purpose.

⮮ REVISIT DEMOCRACY – A PARTICIPATIVE THING

McKnight shows us how professionals and institutions have occupied and continue to annexe the caring territory that is , in the context of real inclusion and belonging , the natural stamping ground of family, friends, neighbours and the wider community – the locus for caring for each other and, I would argue, the seedbed of meaningful, participative politics. Democracy is witnessed when people come together to address common needs and aspirations. Representative democracy might be described as a necessary evil but its more ethical practitioners might adopt the role of encouraging its participatory form at every opportunity?

⮮ IN REDEFINING THE ROLE OF GOVERNMENT BE CLEAR ABOUT WHAT IS 'LOOSE AND TIGHT'

Please be clear that this is not a libertarian treatise. There are many areas of public interest where government needs to be interventionist and clearly in control. Similarly, there are lots of areas of life where the markets do a reasonable job and well designed systems deliver smooth operations and high levels of safety. None of us would want our newsagent at the controls of our holiday Airbus or our neighbour tapping our cerebrospinal fluid, unless of course they are appropriately qualified and experienced. These observations are strictly functional and concerned with what works best, constitutes best use of limited resources, and is sustainable. Above all it is concerned with delivering an achievable and sustainable vision of a kinder and less alienated society.

My simple mind tells me that I've experienced an increasing loss of societal cohesion during my lifetime that directly correlates with the professionalisation of caring roles. If we are going to reverse this trend – and economic realities may add impetus to our need to do this – policy makers have to revisit their assumptions and probably unconscious beliefs about the beneficence of services. We need to reappraise the role of government *vis-à-vis* the role of citizens and ensure that government only intervenes via services and professions where this contributes clearly to a truly felt vision of a society to which we commonly aspire. Our society is people. We are not dispensable drones. We need to give our gifts. We grow in our relationships with each other. And both individuals and society benefit immensely when government and policy makers attend to protecting and liberating these gifts and assets.

So, in summary, we can make a start if we:
- ❖ **FIND OUT WHAT REALLY MATTERS**
- ❖ **LEAD BY EMPOWERING AND STEPPING BACK**
- ❖ **REIN IN THE SOCIAL CARE BUREAUCRACY AND COLONISING PROFESSIONS**
- ❖ **ACCEPT THAT THE STATE CANNOT 'CARE'**
- ❖ **IT CAN DELIVER EXCELLENT SERVICES BUT MUST BE CAREFUL NOT TO TRY TO 'DO THE LIVING FOR US'**
- ❖ **ACKNOWLEDGE THE MISERY OF LONELINESS AND ISOLATION – MAKE 'NO-ONE ALONE' A WEATHERVANE POLICY**
- ❖ **HONESTLY REVIEW AND ACT UPON OUR**

EVALUATION OF THE PROS AND CONS OF THE SOCIAL CARE 'MARKET' – REBALANCE THE COMPROMISES IN FAVOUR OF THE SERVICE USER – FULL BLOWN SELF-DIRECTION IS A GOOD START (ASSUMING THE VESTED INTERESTS DON'T SABOTAGE IT)

❖ ATTEND TO NURTURING SOCIETY, REVITALISING COMMUNITIES, PUTTING THE POWER AND RESPONSIBILITY BACK WHERE IT BELONGS, WITH CITIZENS

❖ TAKE A LONG, HARD LOOK AT SAFEGUARDING – IT DOES TAKE A VILLAGE TO RAISE A CHILD AND HARD CASES MAKE BAD LAW – TRY REACTING FROM A 'GLASS HALF-FULL' PERSPECTIVE

❖ REDEFINE AND RECOGNISE OUR ASSETS

❖ BACK PEOPLE BEFORE SYSTEMS

❖ ENCOURAGE CREATIVE THINKING AND CONTROVERSY

❖ MAKE PERSONAL RESPONSIBILITY AND SELF-DIRECTION A REALITY

⬥ IT'S ALL ABOUT CREATING AND SUSTAINING A BALANCE – PRESENTLY WE'RE OUT OF KILTER.